finally,

A PIECE OF PEACE

"Your safe space to pause, laugh, reflect, and finally, breathe."

finally,

A PIECE OF PEACE

a practical guide for navigating
relationships, balancing emotions,
and becoming yourself

JA'MARA WASHINGTON

Published 2026.

Published in the United States of America

5 ISBN 979-8-9927458-0-1 (print)

ISBN 979-8-9927458-1-8 (ebook)

LC Record available at https://lccn.loc.gov/ (LCN # 2026903120)

Cover design by Tess McCabe

Layout design by Julie Plasse

Copy edited by Courtney Allen

Proofread by Robin Schroffel

Author photo by Alexis Akarolo

First paperback edition March 2026

To my best friends, Cortney and Nathalie.
Thank you for always reminding me to
choose life,
choose joy,
and most importantly,
choose myself.
In every lifetime and on every timeline, I choose you.
Thank you for giving me a piece of peace.

peace

[pēs] *noun*

freedom from disquieting or
oppressive thoughts or emotions

MERRIAM-WEBSTER DICTIONARY

CONTENTS

AUTHOR'S NOTE

Every time I searched for peace, I found words. I found a string of words promising to heal or save me. Some brought me out of dark spaces, while others pulled me deeper into the depths of my pain. In every situation, words changed the trajectory of my life. Whether I wanted them to or not.

My late twenties to early thirties were filled with change—friendships beginning and ending, family passing away, switching careers, becoming an entrepreneur, and moving cross-country. Some I expected, but many I didn't.

Over time, I learned that change was the only constant. So, I committed to learning how to regulate my emotions when the unexpected happened. For six years, my life became about understanding my actions and reactions. With every new situation, I leaned into gratitude and appreciation. Through venting with friends, finding solutions with my therapist, and practicing boundaries in safe environments, I became my most authentic self.

While difficult times still occurred, they didn't last. I finally had the tools, language, and community to navigate any storm. That was my reality—for years. Then, January 2025 entered the chat.

I was in Miami, FL, celebrating my thirty-third birthday. I spent the weekend doing all of my favorite things—visiting coffee shops and art museums, writing this book, eating at Vapiano, and biking along South Beach. Although I was alone, I felt at peace.

I thought about all I had been through to get to that point. Specifically, how I had been on God's strongest soldier list for years. I thought, *No.* I believed all of my pain and confusion had a purpose. It had to mean I was about to step into my best year yet—my "Jesus Year." Although my friendships had ended, my job situation had become unstable, and I was building a new community from scratch, a double blessing was on the way. I truly believed that. But I didn't know that when I proclaimed thirty-three as my Jesus Year, it would get worse before it got better.

On January 12, my birthday, I received news that caused me to walk away from two of my best friends. Friends that I'd had for over a decade. The foundation of my relationships crumbled. And so did I. On a day when I should have been celebrating new beginnings, I was picking up the pieces from messy endings. The desire to celebrate overcoming hard times seemed silly as I found myself in another one. I went back to the hotel and slept the remainder of the night. I needed a break from life.

The next morning, I decided to grab breakfast on South Beach. I thought, *If I can just be next to the water, hear the waves, and feel the breeze, my spirit will settle.* So, I sat on a patio across from the beach. I was close, but not close enough. As I walked down to the pier in my white button-up, denim pants, and Nike color-block shoes, I felt the weight of my reality getting heavier and heavier. I plopped down in the sand, fully clothed and fully broken.

The ocean moved back and forth along the shoreline as if it was breathing: slowly inhaling what was left on the coast, holding its contents still for just a moment, then exhaling what remained as crashing waves. It never worried about what was in the way. It just moved freely. In and out.

I watched the water keep this pattern for a while. As it breathed, I breathed. "Inhale for one, two, three, and four. Hold. Exhale for five, six, seven, and eight. Relax." Just as my yoga teacher had taught me. Yet, something was different. I could no longer keep pace with the ocean. Every time I inhaled, water would fill my eyes. When I paused, I would choke up. On my exhale, my chest would collapse into itself. I could no longer be one with Mother Nature. I couldn't flow as easily as she could. I was different.

Holding onto the only things I could feel—the warmth from the sun above me and the gritty sand beneath me—I wept. I let my emotions have their way with me, only pausing when someone was close enough to see the tears smearing makeup down my face. I, by all accounts, was unwell.

My spirit was broken. I couldn't understand how this could happen. I kept replaying a conversation I'd had with God on New Year's Eve. I told Him, "I don't want to have to beg people to show up for me next year." And within weeks, He revealed that my best friends were the people I was begging the most. Not random strangers, but those I loved more than anyone else. I was devastated. I got what I asked for, but it wasn't what I asked for. Regret was settling in.

As I released my grip on the warm sand, I began to realize that relationships are really hard and *extremely* painful. Even if I was vulnerable, intentional, and supportive, people could still let me down. Those closest to me could still hurt me, even if it wasn't on purpose. It shocked me. I *never* imagined a world where I was hurt. By my best friends? At this age? It had never crossed my mind. But there I was, experiencing first-hand how my strongest relationships could fail.

I got back home to Washington, DC, with more questions than answers. I kept thinking, *What is the purpose of building relationships if I'm just going to be let down? What is the purpose of being vulnerable with people if I'm just going to be left feeling alone?* As I contemplated the meaning of life, I realized the frequency of loss left me emotionally exhausted.

Honestly, it left me feeling hopeless, an overwhelming emotion that sent me into depression. I thought a couple of therapy sessions, yoga classes, and vacations with my friends and family would bring me back to myself. But they didn't. Instead, the slightest inconvenience made me feel as if I was back at square one. Over time, I got tired of feeling as if I was in a never-ending fight with my life, my emotions, and thus, my peace. I wanted a solution that made me feel as if I could finally breathe again.

I started by figuring out what was already giving me peace. Outside of the self-care activities, what was I holding onto when things got hard? It was words. Specifically, affirmations.

Even as I write this, they have such a powerful way of making me feel seen and understood. When I'm in the valley, they make me feel as though I've found the last helping hand on earth. When I'm emotionally overwhelmed, they feel like the warmest hug. But at the *right* moment, affirmations feel like whispers from God—like subtle, but timely, reminders that bring me back to three truths:

1. He knows.
2. I'm not alone.
3. It's okay.

Whenever I'm feeling misunderstood, lonely, or anxious, those truths negate the emotions that leave me feeling stuck or depressed. They allow me to release the thinking that I should be or feel anything other than what I am at the moment. They invite me to speak my own truth:

"I felt the way I did because I didn't have the tools, language, or emotional capacity to handle what was coming my way. That's normal and okay. Today, I affirm there is more *to* me and *for* me. Whatever I'm seeking will find me, too, waiting with open arms and an open heart."

Affirmations. Language. That's how this book was formed. When I started trying to pick up the pieces of my new reality, I dug through old journals and therapy notes, searching for tools, resources, or encouraging words to get me through. I needed something—anything, really—to hold on to. And I found it. While documenting the affirmations that comforted me when life got hard, I found peace.

I realized that I was not a collection of what people had done *to* me; I was a witness of what God had done *for* me. In my journey of beginnings, endings, and messy middles, God has showered me with community. He has placed people in my life who have taught me love, purpose, self-worth, vulnerability, communication, and accountability. Through them, I learned to become more myself. I learned that the way to live a good life is to let others in. Let them show you who you are, speak life into your situation, and support you when you really don't want to be seen.

While it was relationships that broke me, it was also relationships that saved me. And that's not irony, that's divine purpose. There were people and situations that let me down, while there were others that showed me why it didn't matter. I wasn't being broken; I was being moved into alignment. I was being taught *how* to heal; how to stop getting in the way of what, and who, was for me in my current season of life. It was a constant prayer I'd return to throughout my thirties.

I prayed to be loved, aligned, and free. Oof. With everything in me, I wanted to be free. I wanted to put down the never-ending expectations and responsibilities to be someone other than who I was or *wanted* to be. I desired—no, I craved— rest from the facades I didn't even know I was creating. I wanted to rest in my truth, with my emotions, and within my communities. To me, that was peace. *That* became my dream.

And my community helped me live that dream. They helped me carry my load when it became too much for me. Because there were things that occurred that I couldn't plan for. Which brought up emotions I wasn't ready for. After everything fell apart, I realized I'd lost the emotional and physical capacity to handle change. That's why the slightest inconvenience would send me spiraling. It left me feeling more negative emotions than positive ones.

This book explores those difficult emotions. It explores how we navigate relationships and life when they come up. Then it gives us permission to take what we need and leave what no longer serves us. Above all, it gives us the freedom and peace we have been desperately longing for. And it does so with a bit of "kiki" in between the hard truths.

I'm grateful to share what I've learned about self-discovery, relationships, and emotional well-being with you. It's my hope that this will guide you to the safest place you know: **yourself**. And once you become more aligned, I pray you will use this book as a staple in your wellness journey. Let it be a transformative, but practical, resource in your book clubs, wellness retreats, and safe spaces near and far.

I leave my favorite work of art with you—in good hands.

All my love,

Ja'Mara

INTRODUCTION

Words changed the way that I breathed. They gave me freedom from the thoughts that kept me up at night and space to release the emotions I had carried for far too long. When I was searching for peace, words gave me permission to exhale.

But in 2025, I found myself holding my breath again. I was overwhelmed by change. I kept pretending to be okay, doing what so many women do—putting one foot in front of the other while quietly hoping to see the other side of emotional overwhelm. I was tired—exhausted even. I didn't have much to give my family, friends, or self. By February, I was at the end of my rope.

Then, words found me again. A gentle whisper and reminder from long ago:

"You can put the bags down."

It felt as though someone had opened a window in a room I didn't know I was trapped in. It was something my therapist had said to me years ago and reminded me of often. Whenever I felt over-whelmed by life, she reminded me that I could put the bags down.

As women, we are taught to pick up what others drop. To hold emotions that aren't ours. To carry burdens quietly, graciously, and without question. But at that moment, I was handed per-mission: to rest, release, and stop trying to hold a life that wasn't meant to be.

For the first time in a long time, I was offered a piece of peace.

Peace felt like an invitation to put down the expectations I had picked up out of obligation instead of love. It felt like clarity. Like a proposal to experience life the way it was supposed to *be* all along. When I experienced peace, I realized I wasn't meant to exist in spaces I'd outgrown. I was meant to flow—in alignment. It was a fresh awakening that became my daily prayer.

And maybe you're praying for the same thing. Maybe you're dream-ing of a life where familial responsibilities, relationship expec-tations, and corporate ladders don't swallow you whole. A reality where choosing yourself isn't a selfish act but a self-preserving one. The permission to release the emotions that weigh you down so you can heal, feel, and simply *exist*.

If that's the life you're craving, I want to help you get there. When you're tired of being everything for everyone, I want to help you find your piece of peace, too.

Through honest stories, lessons learned the hard way, and prac-tical steps you can take right now, I'll help you understand your emotions, communicate your relational needs, and move through the world as your full, authentic self.

What Is This Book About?

This is about you, and your journey back to freedom. I share my story as a mirror of our shared experiences, collective struggles, and dreams of becoming who we truly are, but this is truly about you.

This book explores how you see yourself, how others see you, and who you're meant to become when those truths finally align. It invites you into the beauty and complexity of romantic, professional, familial, and platonic relationships while teaching you to balance the emotions that come with them, including doubt, anger, grief, and resentment.

While it's filled with thirty affirmations, it's not an affirmations book. A quote can make you feel seen, but it doesn't offer you the chance to see *how* you arrived at your current situation. It can only speak to how you feel after you're there. This book helps you understand the *why* behind your emotional habits and gives you the tools to rewrite them.

It acts as a guide to help you become your authentic self. When you learn more about the world within you, you are better able to show up in the world around you. That is how you find freedom. That is how you experience peace: through alignment.

Whenever you face emotional overwhelm, strained relationships, or never-ending responsibilities, this will be your truth. This will be the way you come home to yourself—again and again.

Why Should You Listen to Me?

I have been there. I have been through it, more than once. I spent the past six years seeking professional and personal help on navigating life—because it's not easy. In my darkest storms, my community shared encouraging words that got me through difficult situations and seasons.

The situations? Well, how about when:

- I spent my entire college career studying a major that I only did because others told me I would be good at it.
- I moved away from my hometown and state without a job or any money.
- I bet my life on an on-and-off-again relationship that didn't work out.
- I lost a parent.
- I struggled with the responsibilities and expectations of being the eldest daughter.
- I discovered therapy, boundaries, people-pleasing, and trauma bonding.
- I found my dream career and switched roles during the pandemic.
- I developed imposter syndrome in that dream career.
- For eight years, I was the only one at work who looked like me.
- I found out the guy I was dating all summer actually had a girlfriend.
- I moved across the country for the second time, chasing a new life.
- I was diagnosed with a hormonal disorder six years after displaying symptoms.
- My relationships with my best friends ended, back-to-back.

Do I really need to go on? I've been there. And through it all, I found strength in these words from those alongside me. That's what I'm sharing with you: the wisdom of my community and the space to finally put your bags down.

What Will You Learn?

Your story won't be identical to mine. That's okay. I didn't write this for us to trauma bond. I wrote this so you could name your emotion, say how you truly feel, and release it without shame.

There will be times when you say, "I haven't been through that situation, but I know that emotion. I've had those feelings, too. And I'm ready to come out on the other side."

This is how. In this intimate journey, you will see different versions of yourself—the one you share and the one you hide. Together, we'll go beyond your titles, responsibilities, regrets, and shame so you can find the version of you that is ready for peace. The one that is ready to move into alignment. And after all these years, the one that is ready to come home.

You will learn to:

1. **Build Your Tools.** So you can understand your emotions, distinguish between what drains you and what restores you, and set boundaries that honor your peace.

2. **Strengthen Your Language.** So you can communicate clearly, navigate conflict, define your limits, and express what you need without guilt.

3. **Expand Your Capacity.** So you will have physical, emotional, and spiritual space for life, instead of feeling weighed down by it.

By the end of this book, you will move into deeper alignment with yourself. Every affirmation comes from real emotions, questions, and revelations. Use them as evidence that you are not alone. Use them to have open conversations about your feelings, emotions, and self-discovery. Then, use them to see yourself clearly and compassionately. You are worth the love and grace you so easily give to others.

This is your permission.

How Should You Read This Book?

There's no right or wrong way to move through these pages. While some stories overlap in time, this book isn't arranged chronologically. Instead, it's organized by the emotions you might be struggling with and are seeking to balance. Each chapter focuses on an emotion and offers a collection of affirmations to help you balance that emotion. Each affirmation shares:

- **A Personal Experience** – This is the why, the moment that inspired the affirmation.

- **An Application** – This is the how, a reminder of its purpose and how to apply it to your life.

- **An Exploration** – This is the if, questions to help you reflect and decide whether this affirmation belongs in your life, too.

You can read affirmations from different chapters, picking what resonates in the moment, or by chapter, focusing on a single emotion you need help with. Take whatever calls to you. This is your journey, your safe space, to pause, laugh, and reflect. Don't worry about having the perfect start. Just start.

You're ready.

one

OVERCOMING SELF-DOUBT

when you feel you are not enough

Society often tells you that you must become or achieve something to be seen as valuable. And after a while, you start to believe it. You start measuring your progress against people who seem to have it all—money, purpose, and affection from others.

While you are happy for the success of your friends, family, and even strangers, you wonder when it will be your turn, or why it didn't come as easily or quickly for you as it did for them. You're questioning whether it was because you weren't talented, rich, or pretty enough.

While those feelings are valid, the narrative around them may not be. You don't have to *be* or *do* anything to be enough. You already are enough—even as you grow, wait, and heal.

Here are some affirmations you can cling to when self-doubt creeps up.

* * *

No one can make you feel inferior without your consent.

ELEANOR ROOSEVELT

When you lose faith in others, sometimes the impact is losing faith in yourself. You lose confidence in your ability to make the right decisions. Which can lead to your seeking a second opinion to validate who you are or what you know to be true.

I get it. In 2011, I felt the most alone and lost. I was starting my sophomore year of college when I found myself picking up my confidence, integrity, and emotions off the floor from a messy friendship breakup. For the first time, I was being perceived by people in a negative light. I became increasingly insecure about my relationships and purpose. I didn't know who I was outside of the communities in which I existed. Nor could I handle the pain from people who knew me best, saying things as if they didn't know me at all. The trust that had once kept my connections—and me—feeling safe faded. To protect my character from further damage, I spent most of the fall semester isolated, just praying for change.

The next semester, change arrived.

My homegirl was concerned about me spending another six months alone, so she invited me to go to an interest meeting with her. I didn't think anything of it. I was a nursing major attending a professional business fraternity event. I was there for moral support. The fraternity hosted a week of events and invited a group to pledge in the upcoming semester. As luck would have it, I, the person who was not interested, was selected over the person who was.

When I received my bid, I was hesitant about being around others again. I was already unsure of myself. I didn't see how I could add any value to anyone, considering the state I was in. But I ultimately took their selection as a sign from God. It was time to face my fears.

As part of the process, I was assigned a mentor to support me throughout my twelve-week journey. Every week, I learned about the organization's history and need-to-know business skills, such as interviewing using the STAR method, giving a thirty-second elevator pitch, or presenting one's resume to potential employers. As a nursing major, these skills were foreign to me. As a first-generation college student, they were also the furthest from my mind. But the fraternity kept them at the forefront. They had checkpoints where members, also known as the brotherhood, would test our knowledge on these skills. After a few short weeks in, I was at my first checkpoint.

I was so nervous. My brain was firing off. *I don't know what I'm doing. What did I get myself into? Is anyone else sweating in their suit?* (It was black, but I could feel the sweat stains forming.)

Typically, mentors would leave gift boxes in the waiting room to prepare their mentees for the evening ahead. They included snacks, a note from their mentor, games to pass the time, and other professional stationery, including pens, resume paper, calendars, and notebooks. My mentor, Jazz, left all my favorite things with a handwritten note. On the outside of my card was a quote I'd never seen before:

No one can make you feel inferior without your consent.

My first thought was, *This can't be Franklin's girl hitting us with the truth we didn't ask for, but absolutely needed!* (Before you ask, yes, I speak about people I don't know as if they are my first cousin. Keep up.)

My second thought was, *How did Jazz know I was feeling like this? We only met a few weeks ago, and now she thinks she knows me? Because maybe she does.* (Picture me ugly crying in a professional setting.)

In my card, she explained that I was going through a new process and doing new things. While I might be anxious about my interview questions and feeling underqualified in a room full of professionals, I *needed* to know that the interviewers were just people. They were neither above nor below me. They were beside me as equals.

I didn't realize it then, but she was teaching me what it meant to be powerful. She was teaching me how to harness power, but also how to get it back if I ever felt I'd lost it.

My nerves started to settle. I thought, *She's right. No one knows what I am going to say, so why am I so concerned that others will perceive my answers as wrong?* But I couldn't think about it for too long. My name was being called to meet my interviewers.

My guide stood in front of me and asked if I was ready to go. I nodded. As I followed her out the room, I kept repeating Eleanor's quote to myself. "No one can make you feel inferior without your consent. No one can make you feel inferior without your consent. *No one can make you feel inferior without your consent!*"

I was still nervous, but I felt ready.

The room was dimly lit and filled with people. I couldn't make out any familiar faces. On my left was a table of three interviewers. On my right was a room full of members from the brotherhood. I rubbed my sweaty palms together and faced the interviewers.

The panel introduced themselves and jumped right into business. "Tell me about yourself." Internally, I let out a deep sigh. I hated that question. Mostly because they were looking at my resume yet asking me something they could see. Partially because the only time I saw that question come up was on my social media. Yet I had a feeling they weren't asking about my favorite music, color, or hobbies. I smiled and gave them my best answer.

The questions continued, each getting more difficult than the last. I felt self-doubt creeping back in. I wasn't getting any confirmation on whether I was answering the questions right. I was hoping for a smile, a nod . . . something. Instead, I was met with blank faces and more questions.

I felt my body getting warm. Was I blushing or sweating again? I didn't know. I took a deep breath and recalled Eleanor's words: "No one can make you feel inferior without your consent." Gratitude for that reminder rushed over me. I was waiting for the next question when I heard, "Miss Washington, please turn to face the audience. Someone has a few words they want to share before you leave." I didn't know what was going on, but I slowly turned around to face my fate.

"Hey, Little," a voice said in a warm and assuring tone.

By the time I'd turned around, I was overwhelmed with emotions. It was my mentor, Jazz! I was shocked she was there. I hadn't seen her in the crowd. (Granted, I couldn't see anything beyond the fear in my own eyes.) Her presence grounded me.

"Hey, Big," I replied with tears in my eyes.

Her smile lines deepened.

She expressed her excitement to be my mentor and go on this journey with me. (Hearing that was comforting. I was scared, but I didn't feel alone.) Then, in a room full of people, Jazz affirmed my worth, talent, and power. She spoke life into me.

I remember thinking, *How can she be so sure of who I am if I don't know who I am?* But she was. From the moment she met me, she saw me. She saw someone who genuinely cared—about and for others. Even when I doubted my character, she didn't. And she wasn't going to allow anyone, including me, to doubt the greatness that was within me. The magic that had always been there, waiting to be acknowledged and released. She proclaimed who I was as an intro for others and a reminder for me.

I started sobbing uncontrollably. (Because What. A. Woman!)

The panel asked me to turn around. They thanked me for my time and dismissed me from the room. As my guide led me back to the waiting area, she turned around and asked if I was okay. With a snotty nose and shaky voice, I replied, "Yeah." We walked a few more steps, and she turned around again. "The interviewers couldn't give you immediate feedback, but you did amazing on your interview questions. There's no need to cry." Once again, I was reassured of my abilities and comforted along my journey.

If you find yourself questioning whether you are good enough for people or opportunities, doubt may have you in a chokehold. Don't let it. Doubting yourself, your abilities, or your results is giving away your power. It is giving consent to others to make you feel less than, when you're not. You are more than capable. You are more than worthy. You are more than enough—yesterday, today, and tomorrow. You're the best they've ever had. If you ever forget that, here are two things that you can do:

1. **Find a trusted opinion.** This can be a friend, family member, or partner. Ask them, "Based on what you know or perceive about me, do you think (negative thought) is true?" For example: Do you think I avoid hard things? Do you think I avoid conflict? Do you think I am untrustworthy? They will likely affirm that you are doubting yourself or your abilities. Then they will give you evidence that you already have a positive experience relating to the "thing" you are doubting. This type of assurance can be a reminder that the tools you used in the past can be used again.

2. **Find an affirmation.** This book contains thirty affirmations to meet you where you are. Read through them. Some will give you language for how you feel, while others will give you answers on how to move forward. Pick your favorite. Commit it to memory. Then, lean on the words from an outside opinion to help you build your confidence.

You got this.

Affirmation: No one can make you feel inferior without your consent.

Application: Draw back to this affirmation when you are nervous about an outcome or potential response. Use it to remain rooted in the fact that the person in front of you is just like you. They are likely just as nervous as you are. Take comfort in that. Like you, they have emotions, doubts, and fears. Inform your nervous system that the person on the other side of you is your equal. They are not above or below you; they are the same as you. When you do this, you remove the pressure to be anything other than your authentic, confident self.

Exploration:
1. What experience are you going through that makes you feel inferior to your peers?

2. What about you is not enough, normal, or correct?
3. Who told you this?
    a. If it was yourself, are you counting yourself out before others can count you in?
    b. If it was someone else, do you give them the authority to speak this over your life?
    c. If it was multiple people, is this feedback you want to adopt or improve on?
4. What do you need to hear or know to become more confident in yourself?

* * *

Everybody else is 2s and 3s. You're the 1.

KURUPT

Being the "only one" in an environment can lead to imposter syndrome. It can lead to doubting your ability, choices, and value. Those doubts showed up the most when I was the only woman or Black person in an organization.

When I moved to the Bay Area in 2016, I was in the underrepresented group everywhere I went—the grocery store, restaurant, shopping mall, and even the beauty supply store. Yes, girl, the beauty supply store. In my first six months, I could count on one hand the number of times I saw someone who looked like me. And this didn't change when I entered Big Tech in 2020, either.

My first tech role was a project manager on a security marketing team. Now, I didn't have a background in security or marketing, so I had some doubts. Not about my ability to excel in the role. I knew I was going to knock it out of the park. But I was second-guessing whether ramping up on the team, security terminology, and mar-keting tools was going to be too much. Would I still be successful when I added all of these new factors? I was still working on a startup when I accepted this role, so I was worried about burning out too quickly. But I thought if God brought me to it, He would also bring me through it.

And He did. While I was the only Black person in that organization, the level of support and respect I received made me feel as if I belonged and mattered to my team. One time, a coworker escalated a concern that the work I was doing was interfering with his team's work and time. My manager and director immediately set up a call with me. They asked me to describe how a recent interaction had gone. They wanted all of the details. What did I say? What did I do? Did I send any emails afterward? They followed up by sending an email to the coworker, reminding him that I was doing exactly what they had hired me to do. And he was failing to complete his part of the project. For once, I didn't have to overexplain my side. I felt supported by my team and validated in my work. And if I'm honest, a little vindicated too, like, "Ha-ha, you thought your efforts would get me fired, but really it just highlighted how you are a bully and not doing your job!"

From then on, I felt like maybe, just maybe, I belonged in Big Tech. Even if I was the only Black person on my team, there was a place for me in spaces where I typically felt othered. As I continued to gather evidence, I gained confidence.

Six months later, I was working at another tech company with hard-ware security engineers—another first for me. This time, I was the only non-technical person on a technical team of 120 people. That meant I was the only person on my team without an engineering degree or position. I was surrounded by experts.

Since I didn't know anything about hardware engineering, I felt as if I was cosplaying as "smart." And though I'd spent a few months on a security marketing team, I wasn't an expert in security. I was scared they were about to find out I was an imposter. Then, regret their decision to hire me. Doubt was settling in—again.

It's weird because I was the go-to person for schedules, process flows, and system integration, yet there were times when my "oneness" made me doubt my skills and abilities despite the evidence.

For example, I was in a technical meeting, and one of my coworkers asked me, the new hire leading the meeting, for more details about our product. (Girl, jump scare!) I didn't have an answer! Really, I had no idea what they were talking about. So, I felt like a fraud. *Look at me, a seasoned business professional, faking my technical readiness on a technical team. Girl, you're going to get fired.* Or so I thought.

Three months later, I was asked to lead a highly visible project with people inside and outside the company. In other words, I didn't have time to fake it. It was the playoffs, and I was the star quarterback. The idea that I didn't belong or was underqualified could no longer exist. It *had* to be a myth. Why? Because my team was looking to me to run the winning play. Not really, but they were looking to me for direction for the project.

So, I had to become what I thought I wasn't before I was. My imposter syndrome was telling me that a non-technical person did not have value or influence on a technical team. It wasn't true, but I had to act like it wasn't to believe it.

First, I had to learn not to be afraid of the technical, unknown, and unexpected questions. So, I learned the art of delegating questions live. I would say, "Let me take a note of that and have someone on the team follow up with you offline," or "Our lead architect is on the line. Yusef, can you take this one?"

Then I learned to get on my Zoom. (Not literally, but figuratively.) If I was going to be an asset on a technical team, I had to learn what I was talking about. So, I set up informational meetings with our engineers to learn more about the product and what kind of issues could come up if we did or didn't do something. Luckily for me, I love a backstory, and hardware engineers love to talk about what they do.

Once I learned the language of my team, and how to delegate questions I didn't understand or responsibilities I didn't own, I was in my bag! I was able to produce meaningful work for the team, which gave me stellar reviews and more high-impact projects. As evidence built up, so did my confidence.

A few weeks later, I was sitting at my desk listening to my coworker compliment me on how I had handled a customer meeting. When the call ended, I was shocked! A senior, technical employee complimented *me* on how I led a technical discussion? As I let that moment sink in, it reminded me of when I doubted whether I was a fit for the team. It reminded me of when I doubted whether my technical coworkers would see me as valuable. As I replayed the compliment, my confidence shot through the roof. That's when Kurupt's voicemail in Jhene Aiko's song "Why You Never Call Me" played in my mind. He said,

"Everybody else is 2s and 3s. You're the 1."

This stuck with me because the artist is backtracking all the wrongs of her partner and feeling ashamed. At the end of the song, her friend reminds her of who she is. He reminds her to stop worrying about the things that don't matter. Everything she needs is inside, and beside, her.

(Insert teary-eyed emoji)

"I'm the one!" I said, loudly enough for me to believe it, but quietly enough so no one in the office would think I was crazy. My imposter syndrome faded when I allowed other people's opinions of me to be the evidence.

Here's the truth: It's hard to feel like an imposter when everyone is reminding you that you are that girl. It's even harder when the evidence doesn't match the story you're telling yourself. If your team said they were so happy you joined and you were the perfect person to help them scale the organization, why would you call them liars? If they didn't doubt you, why would you doubt yourself? You wouldn't! Or at least, you shouldn't.

The evidence is there, showing up either as feedback or results, that you are the one. The evidence is proving that the only person doubting you is *you*. There are so many other things you can fill your mind with. Don't let negative thoughts or false data be among them. Instead, turn down the internal noise and give yourself some grace and praise! Girl, you're the one! Not everybody can say that. But you can.

You are a unique being. You stand out even when you are trying to fit in. So naturally, you will have times when you feel out of place. When that happens, remind yourself that the story you are telling yourself is fake news. You're not the "only one." You're *the* one.

Affirmation: Everybody else is 2s and 3s. You're the 1.

Application: Draw back to this affirmation when you are feeling less than. Use it to remain rooted in the fact that what is on the inside of you cannot be replicated. Your talent, experience, and environment all came together to create your unique perspective, behavior, and gifts. Sit with the truth that no one is you and that is your superpower.

Exploration:
1. What scenarios cause you to compare your talents, personality, or situation to others'?
2. What is the same about the situation or person?
3. Now, what is different?
   a. If there are differences, why do you assume the outcome will be the same? Why do you assume that the alternative path is better than yours or that the other person is better than you?
4. Who said your personality or experiences do not lead to favorable results?
5. Why do you believe them?

* * *

You impress people far away. You impact people up close.

UNKNOWN

Character is defined by what people consistently experience with us. But oftentimes, we determine our character by what people say about us. If it's a flaw, we usually push it to the side, thinking, "What do they know?" But if it's positive, we take their words straight to the bank and cash them in. Their praises become our new measure of self. However, character is not solely determined by what people say but by what they can see for themselves. I learned that character is measured by our level of vulnerability and proximity to others. Here's how I found out.

My homeboy was loved by everyone he met. He could make a crowd of people love him within minutes. Everyone, and I do mean everyone, was impressed by him—even me. I wondered, *How does this man get stellar reviews from everyone? What's his secret sauce? Is it his confidence, charisma, or relationships?*

I started paying attention to his actions and words. What I discovered wasn't a secret sauce to do with character. It was something deeper about relationships. Most of his close relationships were long-distance friends from childhood or undergrad. He wasn't close with anyone locally. His friends in the Bay Area were surface-level at best, so a lot of the praise he received was what I like to call "telephone praise reports."

Telephone praise reports are compliments from people after you tell them about your life, lessons learned, or accomplishments. They sound like "You've come so far," "You're so inspiring," "You're so thoughtful," or "Bro, you're changing the game with this!" They are well-deserved praise from people who get it but are never a witness to it. They are curated reports based on what *you* told people you wanted to be praised for—being trustworthy, reliable, honest, etc. But they aren't always accurate depictions of character because people are repeating what you say about yourself, not building first-hand accounts about who you *actually* are.

I found out most people didn't really know my friend—not even the ones who'd known him for years. They knew a version of him but not the one he lived out day to day.

That struck a chord with me because my "community" looked like his! (Jump scare.) I was also a transplant to the Bay Area. Most of my relationships were either brand new or long-distance, so when my friends were praising me, it wasn't because they saw it for themselves. It was because I'd given them a telephone praise report. That made me question whether I was reporting on my ideal self or my actual self. Was I conceited or authentic? And how would I know for sure?

That's when a quote I'd once read finally clicked:

You impress people far away. You impact people up close.

Meaning your friends and family will always be impressed by you. However, if you only surround yourself with people who don't have physical access to you, they—and you—will never know your true self. You won't have an accurate assessment of how your words, choices, and decisions positively or negatively impact people because they aren't close enough to be affected by them. They aren't close enough to see whether you *are* who you say you are. They can only trust that what they hear, or may see on a short vacation, aligns with your daily actions.

As I got older, I worried about truly knowing myself. Am I who I say I am? I had moved away from everyone I knew and loved. As I was meeting new people, I wondered whether the things I said were an accurate depiction of my character. Was I still trustworthy, reliable, punctual, and all the positive things I spent years showing my long-distance friends and family? Or was I praising an older version of me that no longer existed? I could tell someone all day that I was self-aware, but it was only the people who saw me day in and day out who could attest to whether or not I was truly discerning. I could tell my family that I forgave easily, but only the member who wronged me could attest to my ability to give grace. I could tell my friends that I was the hardest-working person at my job, but only my coworkers could speak to my work ethic.

When I am filled with doubt about my perception or character, this affirmation reminds me of the importance of having proximal relationships—friends who can see me frequently and wholly. They are the ones impacted by my actions and character. It was easy to be a good friend when all I had to do was pick up the phone. It was harder when I had to actually show up. My character was defined by those mundane moments of running errands, picking up friends from the airport, and sharing space after they'd had a long week. I was able to see who I really was when I was close enough to have an impact.

If you are doubting your character, build a local community. They're not there only to support you but to see you. The good, bad, and indifferent. They are there to hold up your truth—not in shame but in love. Let them. Let them shape your story instead of just echoing it. By letting people get close to you and know you deeply, you build a community of participants, not just witnesses, who can hold you accountable and apply grace even when you have your doubts.

Affirmation: You impress people far away. You impact people up close.

Application: Draw back to this affirmation when you are questioning whether you are who you say you are. Use it to remain rooted in the fact that your community is there to be a mirror for you, but you can only see that reflection if you are doing life with them. If you are allowing them to observe, support, and comfort you in real time. This doesn't mean that your long-distance friends and family don't have value. It means that it's important to be active in each other's lives. Take the trip to see them, invite them to the mundane events in your life, and show up for each other. Actively see each other. Then, share what you know to be true about each other.

Exploration:

1. Who are you?
2. How do you know that? (Consider the indications that strengthen your idea of self.)
3. Is this praise by your own account or from someone else?
   a. If it was by your own account, when was the last time you received praise from someone else?
      i. What did they say?
      ii. How did they come to know this information?
      iii. Did they witness it firsthand?
4. How did it feel to receive praise for the qualities you might have seen as insignificant?
5. What would it look like to spend more time with your friends or family?
6. How can you share your desires to be an active witness in their lives?
7. How can you ask them to be a witness in yours?

How Do I Overcome Self-Doubt?

Self-doubt is a reminder that you care about how you are perceived by others and yourself. It means that you're curious about your actions or logic. That's not necessarily a bad thing. We should question people and things around us, but when we do this for too long, it can have a negative effect on our confidence.

You overcome doubt when you remember that you are uniquely and wonderfully made. You weren't created to shrink into spaces and identities that were never yours. You were created to take up space—and a lot of it. However you see fit.

Your value isn't measured by timelines, trends, or comparisons. You're not falling behind, missing anything, or needing to prove yourself to anyone. You just need to trust your character, abilities, and power more.

You're the one the company has been looking for. You're the one that man has been praying about. You're the one your ancestors were waiting on. Do you get it? You're *the* one.

So, don't let anyone make you feel inferior or take your power. Stand proud knowing that you have what it takes to overcome any challenge and accomplish any goal. And with the help of your community, you have the capacity to be everything you know you are: that girl!

(Now, hold my hand.)

Show them who you are.

two

OVERCOMING FEAR

when you need help rewiring your inner thoughts

In a perfect world, you wouldn't fear anything. You could see any challenge or hardship and face it with confidence and courage. Unfortunately, that's not realistic. Life can be unpredictable and scary. There are some situations, environments, and people that make you second-guess things. And once the seed of doubt enters your mind, fear can take over.

I get it. I've had many experiences that shook me to my core. I'm not talking about a relationship-ending kind of experience; I'm talking about a fear-for-my-life experience. In those scary moments, I needed something stronger than external validation. I needed internal validation that I was safe and that things were going to be okay—that *I* was okay.

I learned that fear is false evidence appearing real. While the emotion may be real, my belief about what is going to happen may not be. I have the power to write my narrative.

When you need help rewiring your inner thoughts, you can lean on these affirmations to remind you to fear not.

* * *

PTSD is telling ourselves, 'I am never letting this happen again.'

THERAPIST

Whenever something heart-wrenching or painful happened to me, I tended to note all the things that led up to the event to prevent it from happening again. I thought that was how you learned from your mistakes and grew in maturity. It wasn't until I was sitting across from my therapist that I realized not only was that not the case, but I was experiencing post-traumatic stress.

In summer 2023, my friend and I decided to go to Los Angeles for the Fourth of July weekend. We were hopping rooftops, day parties, and all the soul food restaurants with old and new friends. To put it frankly, *Boy, we had a time last night!*

It was the best weekend, until it wasn't.

On July 5, around 1:30 a.m., we were heading back to Inglewood, California, from a night downtown. Fireworks were still going off across the city, and people were out gallivanting.

Our Airbnb was located on a street that looked as if it came straight out of a magazine. It was a quiet neighborhood with spacious homes, long driveways, wide streets, and palm trees that could touch the sky. I thought, *We really lucked out on this location!* We had booked a private suite located on the left side of the one-story home. It was L-shaped, and the private entry led to a sunroom, which had additional doors leading to the bedroom and bathroom. The windows in the bedroom and bathroom overlooked a carport area. It was perfect.

That night, I made a left turn onto the street where our Airbnb was. In the distance, I could see a car in the middle of the road. Initially, I didn't think anything of it. I assumed it was at a stop sign or just an Uber dropping someone off. As I drove down three more streets, I noticed the car was in the same spot—the middle of the road. It didn't sit right with my spirit.

As I pulled up to the house, I looked over at my friend and said, "Let's just grab the food and go inside. Don't worry about our bags. That car is sketching me out." We got out of the car and started walking across the street to the private entrance. Immediately, the car slammed on the gas and started barreling down the street at full speed. I remember yelling at my friend, "Run!" as we heard the engine roar.

I thought the car was going to hit us, or even worse. We ran up the long driveway, not looking back, and frantically tried to punch in the door code. I kept saying, "What is going on? What is going on?" Suddenly, the car stopped. We ran inside, locked the sunroom door, closed the window shades, locked the Juliette doors attached to the bedroom, and bunkered on the floor while carefully peeping out the windows.

My mind started racing with worst-case scenarios. I thought, *They are going to come back! They know which house we are in because it was the only lit-up driveway in the neighborhood!* Then it jumped to, *How are we going to get out of here? Oh, the carport window is broken. We can use that if they come through the front door. Wait, they can use that to get in!*

While I was running through every possible escape route, my friend quietly got ready for bed. It was 2:00 a.m., and he was exhausted. I was too, but my fear left me restless. I could barely keep my eyes closed for thirty minutes without my brain reminding me that every sound I heard could mean life or death. I spent most of the night calculating how much time we had left before we could leave: eight hours until the flight, four and a half hours until sunrise, and four hours until the airport opened. When the sun rose, we grabbed our bags and headed out. Finally, I could breathe again.

As luck would have it, I had a therapy session a few days after getting back to the Bay Area. As I explained what happened (that these folks lost their rabbit ass minds), what I felt (scared beyond belief by abrupt, loud noises, even three days later), and what I believed to be true (I will never return to LA or stay in an Airbnb again), my therapist said to me in a very concerned tone,

"PTSD is telling ourselves, 'I am never letting this happen again.'"

"You are traumatized, which stems from two emotions: 1. This is so much bigger than me, and 2. There's nobody to help me." She explained the chances of feeling both, but that feeling enough of one was enough.

I could go viral for the number of times I ugly cried on Zoom or in person with my therapist. I honestly didn't have any idea how common PTSD was. I thought it was reserved for people who had gone to war or been on the other side of a heinous crime. In that moment, I felt both of those emotions. I noticed that even after I returned home, the sound of tires screeching or unexpected loud noises sent me jumping. I was always looking over my shoulder, even in the comfort of my own home. No matter how "safe" my environment seemed to be, my mind and body didn't believe it.

Over the next few months, I spent a lot of time trying to reassure my psyche that I was safe. I told myself that I wasn't in LA or an Airbnb, so I was okay. But that didn't truly ease my worries. I was trying to give my inner child something to hold on to—a condition that dictated her safety. I'd say, "If you are here and not there, you are safe." That created another belief: that I could only be safe under certain, and specific, circumstances. This perspective kept me in fear for another two years.

As I continued to travel, hotels became my preferred, and only, option for accommodations. As my friends continued to invite me on trips, I continued to respectfully decline invitations to LA. I was too scared. For years, I held onto that deep-rooted belief that certain conditions threatened my safety. That didn't change until I had exposure therapy, a practice that helps to retrain the brain and reduce intense feelings of fear. I released the belief that my mind and body hadn't been able let go.

When 2023 came to an end, I made the decision to move across the country. During that time, many of my friends had moved to LA. I wanted to spend my last few months with the people I cared about most, which meant I had to face my deepest fear: a lack of safety.

By Christmas, I was in LA visiting my guy best friend. We had met in the Bay Area, but stayed connected throughout our cross-country moves. He was aware of my fears and could even relate because he was no stranger to questionable characters and situations. When faced with fear, he would walk through it with confidence and a level head. I always admired that about him: his ability to change. So when I became riddled with fear and a million worst-case scenarios, he assured me that I was safe. To be specific, he assured me that the need to keep my head on a swivel was, in fact, pointless. And the LA I once loved was still lovable. I was safe.

"PTSD is telling ourselves, 'I am never letting this happen again'" is a mantra that reminds me of the depth of my emotions and experiences. When I notice myself bargaining about what I will or won't do, I'm reminded that my experience took a deeper hold than I would like to admit. I may have felt that I didn't have the right resources or people around me to get through, and I likely still feel that way. By acknowledging that the experience was traumatizing me so much that I had to create new habits and beliefs for myself, I was able to acknowledge that my inner child was crying for help—that *I* needed help. And quickly.

I learned that the more honest you are with yourself about where you are (down bad) versus where you're pretending to be (blessed and highly favored), the quicker you can get rid of those conditional beliefs and the sooner you can receive the help you desire.

Affirmation: PTSD is telling ourselves, "I'm never letting this happen again."

Application: Draw back to this affirmation when you experience something that shakes you to your core. Use it to remain rooted in the fact that what happened to you was real, unexpected, and scary. While all those things are worthy of shutting down, you are allowed another version of your story. Fear and gratitude cannot co-exist. So, feel the emotion. Seek help moving it out of your body. Then find someone safe to help you rewrite how the best version of your life could go. Now, live it—regardless of what others tried to take from you.

Exploration:
1. When was the last time you said you would never let something happen again?
2. What happened?

3. Was the incident due to the environment you were in, the people you were with, or a personal decision you made?
4. What emotions came up?
5. Are you constantly reliving those emotions, or did you acknowledge that it happened and move on?
    a. If constant, who could best support you in telling your truth or rewriting your desired version? (It doesn't have to be the same person, and it could be a therapist or trauma-informed coach to help you move the trauma through your body.)

* * *

FEAR: False. Evidence. Appearing. Real.

ZIG ZIGLAR

The mind is a funny thing. Despite your best efforts, it will make you believe that the reality you create in your mind is more real than the one you are living in; more real than the one you are seeing with your own eyes. Once your mind believes it, your heart follows. That's when fear kicks in.

Coco is my best friend. We met in San Jose, California, during a Netflix happy hour in 2019 and have been inseparable ever since. In 2024, we decided to leave the Bay Area for a new adventure. She went down to Los Angeles, and I went to Washington, DC. We promised we would visit every few months. (Because how could we live without each other? I am nothing without my girl. Exaggerating, but only slightly.)

In April 2025, Coco came to DC. She had been to graduate school there, so this was her first time back in a long time. I planned a weekend of all our favorite things—yapping on the couch, at the coffee shop, over dinner, and at a day party. I can't explain it, but it was iconic. Everything about the weekend felt like "I'll do it again." I introduced her to my new friends, and we spent every day going wherever the wind blew. The ultimate dilly dally.

On her last day, we decided to brunch with my homegirl, people-watch at the park, and listen to my favorite DJ on Arlo's rooftop. We got there early and watched the city come alive for hours.

As we were exiting the party to go to another event, we stopped at the DJ booth to see my favorite DJ. Coco was new to DJing and loved to connect with other artists. She started talking with some folks while I went to record the DJ. I was mid-fangirling when I overheard disdain in her voice. She was talking to my homegirl, so I thought nothing of it. After I got my footage, we headed downstairs to catch our Uber. As we were waiting outside the hotel, she said a guy shoved her out the way at the DJ booth while trying to record a group of girls. I said, "Well, that was uncalled for. Nothing is that serious," and got into the car. By this point, we had been outside for nine hours, and everyone was exhausted. We decided to grab dinner and go home.

When Coco and I entered my house, we took off our shoes and jackets. Then we stepped into the bathroom to remove our makeup. I looked in the mirror, let out a sigh of exhaustion, and grabbed a makeup wipe. That's when I heard those four words no one wants to hear from someone they love.

"We need to talk," she said.

Girl, I have to be honest. I looked like a deer caught in headlights. I was shocked because I didn't know we had beef. Didn't we just have an Insecure-coded weekend filled with do-it-for-the-plot moments? How could anything be wrong?

"Okay," I said calmly as I turned around to face her.

She proceeded to tell me she hadn't felt supported at the party. Someone pushed her at the DJ booth, and she was disappointed that I didn't even ask how she was doing. I was pained by her words and confused by the role I had played.

I started questioning myself. *Wait, what happened? I didn't realize. Was I being a bad friend? Was I so caught up in my own world that I wasn't even curious about someone else's? Even if that someone else was the most important relationship for me?* I was hurt by my actions or lack thereof.

She continued explaining.

"I told you someone pushed me, and you didn't ask if I was okay. I just wanted you to know that hurt my feelings. I felt like you knew and didn't care. Someone else asked if I was okay, but you didn't. As my best friend, I expected you to care. I just wanted to let you know how I felt."

Now, this would've sent an older version of me into a tizzy! Conflict? Direct communication? Scared! But this was my fifth year of practicing how to communicate with my friends, so I said the only thing appropriate in that scenario.

"I'm sorry. I never want you to feel like that."

We continued talking about the event and the reason for all of the disappointment. I'd had no idea that someone had put their hands on her *and* it had impacted her so much. Why? Because once her mind concluded, "She doesn't care about me," her heart followed. Her actions followed. She was silent for the rest of the night, only expressing her true feelings once we were alone in the safety of my home.

She was experiencing

FEAR: False. Evidence. Appearing. Real.,

an acronym I learned in therapy. It's the emotion we feel when the thoughts we are telling ourselves outweigh what may be happening. We let fear of what we believe to be true drive our reactions, such as inaction.

It felt right to explain where I was coming from. "I had no idea he put his hands on you! I'm so sorry. I didn't see that. I was consumed by my camera. I wish I had seen it because we would've been fighting in the club. I don't play about you! My Shayla? I'm so sorry. I want to protect you at all costs. When you mentioned earlier what had happened, I assumed it was a personal conversation you were having with our mutual friend. I'm sorry I didn't ask more questions. I had no idea that you felt this way."

"Thank you for saying that. Actually, I'm sorry because I never expressed how I felt. I assumed you were aware and didn't care, so I shut down. I should be apologizing to you. I believed something and ran with it. Thank you for listening to me and confirming that what I thought was happening wasn't happening for everyone," she replied.

We cried and hugged for a while, embracing each other with understanding and compassion. It was yet another defining moment in our relationship and truly a masterclass in building relationships that go the distance.

As we discussed what we felt, what we thought, and what our intentions were, we affirmed that we only wanted the best for each other and, more importantly, we only wanted to *be* the best for each other. What does that look like?

1. **Don't wait to say how you feel.** When something is bothering you, don't wait to bring it up. When you take too long to comb through the data or validate your experience with your friends, you only give your fragile mind ways to support your biased opinion. Why is it biased? Because it's one-sided. You didn't give the other person a chance to give you a complete picture of what happened. Invite them in. Then remember, "Yes. And." *Yes*, what you experienced happened, *and* so did other things that you were unaware of.

2. **Confirm reality.** There is a way to let someone know if something is not meeting your expectations. Let them know the action and the emotion. Avoid blaming them for the way you felt. Instead, inform them how an action led you to feel or think something is true. Allow them to confirm or deny your reality. Invite them into your mind. Multiple things can be true at once.

3. **Apologize quickly.** If you have contributed to an unexpected disappointment or failure and you value the relationship, apologize quickly. Take accountability for the role you may or may not have played in the situation. This diffuses you as the accused and them as the accuser. It's not a manipulation tactic; it's a human connection adjustment. Now that the egos are set aside, you can get down to the resolution, together.

4. **Reset expectations.** The most important factor in conflict resolution is learning more about your brother, cousin, boyfriend, or homegirl. Something happened, and they may express what they would have preferred to happen. That isn't an attempt to tell you how to act or what to do, but their way of telling you what they care about.

My best friend cared about me following up and intentionally taking a second to come into her world. She had wanted to tell me what hurt her but never received the opportunity.

I only know that because she continuously teaches me that there *is* a right way to bring up conflict: tell the other person what you saw, what you were expecting, and how what took place made you feel. No long explanations or justifications. Just the facts. That way, the other person doesn't feel attacked, and y'all can address the problem together.

That day, she reminded me to be an active friend. Sometimes that looks like coaching myself through an interaction. I'll often say, "Ja'Mara, slow down and ask about your friend. They are taking the time to tell you about something that happened. So, ask how that made her feel. At the very least, listen in case she *does* have something to say."

Our mind is a beautiful and scary place. It can create something from nothing, which can lead to new products, businesses, and relationships. It can also loop our worst fears and find evidence to make us think that we are living in them. One leaves you feeling empowered, and the other leaves you stuck. However, we can balance those feelings of doubt by saying the hard things out loud, allowing our friends, family, or spouse to provide more context.

Affirmation: FEAR is: False. Evidence. Appearing. Real.

Application: Draw back to this affirmation when you're not sure what the truth is. Use it to remain rooted in the fact that the truth comes from real-time evidence, not scenarios you made up in your mind or past experiences with different players. You will only be able to determine what is real when you allow your psyche to connect to what's happening in the moment.

Exploration:

1. Are the stories you are replaying based on a two-way conversation or solely your view?
2. What did you want to happen versus what you saw happen?
3. How can you communicate your reality to the other person?
4. If your doubts are confirmed, can you express what emotions you felt and your desires moving forward?
5. Can your desires be met by the other person? (It's their choice if they want to, or can, meet your expectations.)
6. If your doubts were not confirmed, can you apologize to them (if you acted on those doubts) and yourself?
7. Can you give grace to them and yourself for not knowing what you couldn't know without speaking?

* * *

Where's the evidence?

JA'MARA WASHINGTON

I'm convinced that the older we get, the harder it is for someone to tell us anything about ourselves, even if what they're saying holds truth. We live in a world where everyone has opinions about how we live, dress, speak, and so on. To protect our mental health, we often tune those voices out. I get it. I'm the same way. It's hard to know which opinions to absorb and which to ignore. That becomes even harder when the opinions come from close friends or family.

Will had been my best friend since 2014. We built a decade-long friendship rooted in music, laughter, late-night talks, and life milestones. We weren't just close; we were foundational in each other's lives. He was my first guy best friend and the standard for my platonic relationships. So, when a casual conversation turned into a sharp critique of my preferences and processes, I was deeply hurt.

It was December 2024. I was in Orlando for a winter dinner that my homegirl was throwing. She invited us after recently meeting Will. It wasn't far from his house, so I thought it would be the perfect way to celebrate our tenth year of friendship. We spent the night dancing to dancehall, eating Jamaican food, and sweating off the liquor in our nice clothes. It was the perfect evening.

The next morning, Will and I had a heartfelt conversation in his kitchen. For hours, we marveled at how much life had changed. Mostly, how *we* were different. We talked about the new aspects of our personalities and how, over time, our ideas about love, dreams, and ourselves had changed. It was beautiful and profound to see us extending grace to our younger selves. That conversation spilled over to the rest of our day plans: brunch, the bar, and later dinner. We decided to get a to-go order from his favorite Jamaican spot.

As we pulled up to the house, an artist that we both enjoyed played through the car speaker. We jammed in the garage for a bit before he asked whether I'd heard Leon Thomas's full album. I mentioned that I had but I didn't care for it. He was shocked and challenged my take by naming his favorite songs. We listened to one, and I was bobbing my head to it. I said, "I see why you like it. I'm going to add it to my Spotty." Again, he was shocked by my comment. He talked about how it was a good song and went into the artistry behind Leon's music. This was typical of our relationship. After all, our shared love of music is what sparked the friendship in the first place.

After his spiel, I suggested we go inside because the oxtail aroma was turning my stomach in the best way. I was ready to eat, so I sat at the kitchen counter and popped open my plastic container.

While he was grabbing drinks and napkins, I replayed Leon's album. I thought, *Maybe I missed something?* As for me and my house, it only takes about fifteen seconds to know if a song is going to move me or not. I was going through the track list when he asked why I wasn't playing the whole song.

"I don't need to. That's not how I listen to music."

"That's what I hate about this generation. You rush through things," he interrupted.

I looked at him in confusion. We were only a few years apart.

"That's not the *only* way you listen to music!"

I explained that it was. "I only add songs that remind me of a feeling, moment, or person."

"No, it's not. Not every song you have in your library is because you can relate to it." He seemed genuinely annoyed with my position on this.

I became more confused. Where was this energy coming from? Why was he so pressed about proving how I did or didn't do something he was watching me do?

"It's okay if we disagree. I don't know why we are arguing about this. It's very strange," I said jokingly, but with increasing concern.

"No, because you are saying there is a specific way you do things when I've seen you do it another way before," he responded.

"Okay. But you asked me about how I listen to music right now, and I told you. You are not accepting what I told you about my process despite watching me do it."

From here, the conversation took a turn for the worse. He brought up things he'd never said before. I was caught off guard as I licked the oxtail gravy off my fingers. He explained how I *never* let him speak during an argument, which was true; I never saw his side of things, and I thought he was dumb . . . Girl, what?

Left field comments! At one point, I just apologized to diffuse the conversation. Then, he accused me of deflecting and shutting down. He was right about the latter. The conversation started going in circles. Then, he stood up and raised his voice.

I was shocked! Because 1. Why are you yelling at a lady? and 2. When did our perfect weekend turn into a blame game?

After ninety minutes, he said the main thing. He was frustrated because he wanted to be able to provide input into my life the same way I provided input into his. He wanted to be a resource for me as I was to him. He explained what he really needed. I empathized with that.

I apologized again and asked, "In the future, could you tell me what you need, versus showing me?"

People tend to show you they are angry, upset, or frustrated rather than telling you their feelings are hurt after something did or didn't happen. This could look like slamming doors, raising their voice, mimicking your statements, etc. It can show up as passive, passive-aggressive, or aggressive behavior.

The question made him even more upset. He felt he was being clear and direct about how he felt, and I wasn't listening. Yet we were on hour two of the conversation, and I still didn't know what the issue was or why he was yelling. And it seemed as if the more I asked, the more anger and blame surfaced.

Girl, I ended up packing my suitcase and leaving. He offered to drive me forty-five minutes to my preferred hotel. I cried the whole way, as he played the same album that had launched us into the argument. It felt like the beginning of the end.

I got into my hotel room and cried some more. I was desperately trying to figure out what had happened and what I could have done differently. *Am I the problem? Am I really someone who doesn't listen to other people's opinions?* I was shocked, heartbroken, and now, spiraling.

I spent years ensuring my friendships were safe places, but in that conversation, I no longer felt emotionally safe. While I updated him on the current version of me, he only wanted to see the old one. I was okay with his differing opinion about my music process. What I wasn't okay with was his tone and accusations. While the blaming made me feel under attack, the constant yelling made me feel unsafe.

I shared a voice note of my feelings, opinion, and desire to continue the relationship despite the high emotions. After all, it was one of the most important relationships to me. I ended the message with, "Call me." The next day, he said he'd call soon.

"Soon" never came. An entire month passed waiting for his call. I wanted to know what had happened, why the conversation had gone left, and where all the energy had come from. I had so many questions. Did he really feel and mean the things he said? Did he *really* view me that way? It felt so misplaced and misdirected.

For thirty days, I wondered,

Where's the evidence?

Where's the evidence that I never do this or that? Is this a blind spot I've always had, and no one said anything? Have I been told this before and never acted on it? Am I so stubborn that I can't hear another opinion that isn't my own? Where's the evidence? He didn't provide any when we talked, and I didn't have any either.

After a month, my thirty-third birthday came around. A text from Will came through.

"Happy birthday. I love you. Enjoy."

I kept reading it, thinking I'd missed a hidden message. I was waiting at 12:30 a.m. for more to be said. But nothing came. Instead, I was left with painful questions. What is love? Is this it? I would never rush someone to speak after having a difficult conversation. I believe you have to let God speak to you, and sometimes a few other people, before you have the language to address what is going on, how you feel, and what you need. But I expected that even if Will wasn't ready to speak or was still finding the words, he would at least reach out to say, "Hey. I haven't forgotten about our conversation. I need more time. Chat soon." Instead, he sent me a birthday message, not even acknowledging our last interaction. Acting as if nothing had happened and everything was good.

Girl, I cried for an hour!

In between responding to other birthday messages, I had to find ways to push aside my pain and make a hard decision. If this *is* love, is this the love I *want*? I'd just moved across the country, again, looking for community; fighting for my friends to show up without me having to ask, beg, and initiate. Did this look like that? The answer was no.

I loved Will and appreciated what we'd built together, but I couldn't receive love like that anymore. I no longer wanted a love that left me in the dark about how they were feeling as they walked back into my life as though nothing had happened. I no longer wanted a love that assumed only their emotions mattered. That their unspoken expectations, or resentment, were valid, so their absence did no harm to the relationship. Not anymore.

When I took a step back, through force or by choice, the evidence found me. The more I looked for examples of how I was in the wrong, the more I saw that this was his pattern. The previous year, he'd had an unspoken pain that led him to avoid reaching out for four months—until my birthday.

Honestly, the more I looked for ways to justify his actions, the more I had to explain my own. Why was I holding onto a relationship I felt neglected in? This wasn't a one-time instance; it spanned years. I had the hardest and loudest arguments with Will. We had ended our friendship many times in the past decade. But at the end of those conversations, we justified them by saying that our experiences made us better, wiser, and more empathetic.

I justified them.

I was reminded of a question David, another best friend, asked me when I was having issues in my romantic relationships. Despite their horrible display of character, I would always create space to listen to their side of the story and rekindle relationships that didn't make sense. He asked me, "Why are you always willing to have a conversation after a harmful situation? What's driving that need? What is it costing you to make space for them?" (Damn Gina! He didn't have to call me in like that. But really, he did.)

I believed that conversations brought understanding, connection, and change. That wasn't always true. And it cost me my time and emotional well-being to make space for people who weren't making space for me. Every time I held the door open, I was unintentionally teaching them that no matter what they did, or how they made me feel, there would always be room for reconciliation. We could talk, and it would be "all good."

Not anymore.

As I said, it's funny how we go through situations that require us to reset our narratives. Sometimes the narrative is about them, and sometimes it's about us. When we feel our character is being attacked or we are being misunderstood, we have to ask: Is there any truth to this? Because sometimes there is, and sometimes there isn't. You will only know when you release your fears and find the evidence.

Here's how you do it:

1. **Ask yourself, "Have I heard this before?"** Something you hear once or for the first time should be taken with a grain of salt. It could be true, or it could be a projection of the other person. It could be something they are working on but not able to communicate yet. There's not enough data to tell, so hear them out, but don't feel compelled to act. If you have heard it more than once and from multiple people, girl, go ahead and take that to the bank. The evidence is evident! It's time to change your actions, tone, or logic.

2. **Ask yourself, "Does this person know the current version of me?"** Sometimes the data you hear is based on an older version of you. It's not who you are, but who you used to be. (That's alright.

Awareness is key.) If you no longer behave or speak in a way your friend, partner, or family member is trying to correct, tell them. "Thank you for letting me know. I noticed that too. I recently changed the way I move, so I don't do that anymore." If they are aware of your current flaws, thank them for telling you. Again, awareness is key. It's scary telling someone things they could do better. Thank them for their courage to say what others wouldn't. Thank them for being vulnerable enough to trust you with data about *you*. (Iron sharpens iron.)

3. **Ask yourself, "Where's the evidence?"** Do you know why they said what they said? Was there a cause and effect? A specific example that supported their concern? If there was, thank them for telling you. Now you know how x could lead to their feeling like y. If they didn't provide any examples, do you have any? Has anyone else given you an example of this same concern? If yes, lean on the evidence and take action. If not, put this information in your back pocket. What's meant for you will always find you. For example, if you receive a comment that you talk over people, there will come situations that either show that you do or remind you not to. Wait for the evidence. Then decide how you want to proceed.

Affirmation: Where's the evidence?

Application: Draw back to this affirmation when you are questioning your reality. Use it to remain rooted in the fact that some statements need evidence. Some assumptions and inferences don't hold as much weight as they could because the person giving you the information doesn't know who you are today. They know a past version of you and need to be reintroduced to your current interests, values, and character. Whether they are your parent, sibling, friend, or partner, update them on who you are today.

Exploration:

1. What characteristics are you questioning about yourself?
2. Has anyone else mentioned you possess these traits?
   a. If so, who and how long have they known you?
3. Do they know the current version of you?
   a. If so, do some further journaling about why you possess those traits and whether you want to continue possessing them.
   b. If not, choose what you want to do with that information.

* * *

Be someone that's living out here.

PRINCE KAYBEE

The pandemic was a time in my life when all I had was time and all I wanted was connection. Like the rest of the world, that connection became Netflix, Clubhouse, IG Parties, and TikTok dance challenges. (Am I showing my age? Whoops! Let's quickly move on.)

I watched a movie on Netflix called *Fetch Your Life*, and it easily became a favorite of mine. The main character was an aspiring South African dancer who waited tables in the day and breakdanced at night. It was the epitome of making your dreams a reality. To really pull my heartstrings, they played *Fetch Your Life* by Prince Kaybee and Msaki. The hook came on and I was dialed in:

> *We live for the weekend working up the courage*
> *We pray away, pray away, pray away*
> *The pain on not being in alignment with our dreams*

Then the chorus:

Fetch your life
Go on be alive
Ain't nobody living out here
Be someone that's living out here

Girl, when I tell you I was in a 360 chokehold, I mean it! I played that song every morning and night for two months straight. It became *my* theme song.

At the time, I was miserable at work. I was applying for my next job while at my current job. But it just left me feeling drained, discouraged, and unmotivated. Then, one day, my coworker, the only other Black woman at the company, told me how she got a Project Management certification. She said it drastically increased her salary and opened opportunities for her. I thought, *Girl, sign me up!*

I left our conversation feeling inspired. I was ready to go after the next chapter of my career. (There's something about getting the blueprint from a Black woman that feels so life-changing!) I quickly bought the prep materials and asked my company to pay for the initial training, which they did. Then I scheduled informational sessions with project managers on LinkedIn to make sure it was something that I really wanted. After everything was set in motion, I learned that I was about to be put on a performance improvement plan at work. (Well, that took a turn.) A performance improvement plan was HR code for "You are about to be micromanaged and fired."

I had two choices:

1. To fight for the job I hated but provided me with security, flexibility, and a steady income.
2. Quit, to be "someone that's living out here."

Girl, I wanted to be someone that's living out here, bad! I wanted to feel aligned and excited about my work. I wanted to be creative, lead teams, and just progress in my career. So, I bet on myself and quit that job. A month later, I passed my certification. Three months later, I landed a role at a major technology company in Silicon Valley.

When I jumped into the unknown, I had no idea what was going to happen, but God did. He put the vision in my heart before I could see the external circumstances that awaited. It's easy to have faith, trust my intuition, and chase my dreams when I can see the end goal. It's easy when I have plans for my plans. It's hard when there are unknowns and I don't know when my next check is coming in. But I did it anyway. I traded comfort for alignment and my calculated plans for faith. And it paid off.

When I look back at that time in my life, I'm incredibly proud. I was so scared back then. I didn't want anyone to see me fail. Everyone was rooting for me. I thought, *If this doesn't work out, how will I recover from such a big risk? I have rent to pay! This money is not growing on trees, nor is this the place where I want to 'f' around and find out.* Luckily, faith took me places fear could not.

Here's the truth: every decision you make is a risk. And as much as you try, you don't know what is going to happen. You have no evidence of what you cannot see; only speculation. So why not speculate that you can live the life of your dreams? Why not have faith that it will all work out if you just go all in? You're betting on your dreams—your livelihood. That type of determination can't be shaken, taken, or broken.

When God puts something down on the inside of you, nothing can stop you from thinking about it. Nothing can stop you from wanting it. Only *you* can. Only *your fear* can. It's okay. It happens to everyone, but you have to decide what to do next: shrink or live.

I hope you choose to live.

The world is *waiting* on you to live.

So, stop playing it safe and do it scared! Fear doesn't have a hold on you. It's a temporary emotion when you feel you're out of options. You're not. The limit does not exist for you. Why? Because what you are chasing is also chasing you. So be someone that's living out here and fetch your life!

Affirmation: Be someone that's living out here.

Application: Draw back to this affirmation when you need a reminder to go after your dreams, even the scary ones. Use it to remain rooted in the fact that everybody is putting on a front to look happy, but few actually *are*. Why not be a part of the select few? Why not be the one who is truly living? Not for social media, the approval of your parents, the notoriety at work or home, but for you. It's time.

Exploration:
1. What does "living" look like to you?
2. What is your latest dream or pie-in-the-sky goal?
3. Are those two answers the same? Do they coexist?
    a. If not, dig deeper to see whether this is a dream of yours or a dream of others.
4. What core emotion do you have around fulfilling your dreams—fear? Excitement?
5. What do you think will happen if this becomes a reality?
6. Are you ready to face that?
7. Are you ready to "live" regardless of what it costs you?

How Do I Overcome Fear?

Fear is not something to eliminate or conquer. It's an emotion you should acknowledge, sit with, and understand. It's your body's way of alerting you to something it perceives as a threat—real or imagined. It's the signal that you care about your safety, well-being, and the outcome of your life. Even when you try to ignore it, your body whispers that something matters. Listen to it.

Acknowledge fear by noticing how it shows up in your thoughts and actions. Are you hesitating more than usual? Avoiding situations or conversations? Playing out worst-case scenarios in your mind as if they're inevitable? These are a few of the ways fear makes itself known. Whether you're afraid of loss, change, failure, rejection, or even success, naming the fear is the first way to honor its presence.

You can sit with fear by resisting the urge to run from it or suppress it. Make space to explore what's behind the fear without rushing to fix it or explain it away. Allow yourself to feel the discomfort, move through it, and learn from it. Sitting with fear doesn't mean letting it control you. It means showing up for yourself in the midst of it, with honesty and compassion.

You don't have to be fearless to be brave. You can be terrified and still take the next step. Whatever you're afraid of, you have the capacity to face it. You don't have to do it all at once. You just have to keep showing up. Only you can decide how to carry your fear—and how to keep it from carrying you.

(Now, hold my hand.)

I'm proud of you for making it this far.

three

OVERCOMING ANXIETY

when you need a reminder to slow down

Sometimes our emotions start as doubt, turn into fear, and settle as anxiety. And let's be honest, that's scary as hell. Unless you've experienced anxiety, it's hard to describe how real, intense, and heavy the emotion feels.

It can feel like an elephant is sitting on your chest or like the weight of the world is on your shoulders. It can show up over things that you don't have time or energy to sort out. It can leave you feeling as if the relationship, job, or sometimes your life, is out of your control.

Anxiety is a scary cycle of worry and fear. One moment you're worried about *how* you're going to make it, and the next moment you're scared about *whether* you will make it. It's a sudden emotion that's hard to explain to friends, family, and even medical professionals. Nothing you describe makes sense. Your vitals are normal, but you don't feel normal. Everyone thinks it's just in your head. They don't get it.

But I do. Anxiety is tough. I still deal with anxious thoughts and feelings sometimes. I learned the way to get through anxiety is to slow down and focus on breathing. This encourages the mind to pause the worrying thoughts and concentrate on moving in a naturally slow, but steady, rhythm.

When you feel that there is too much going on, lean on these affirmations to remind you there is no need to rush. What is going to happen will happen. And it will be in your favor if you release the fear and worry that it won't.

* * *

Wherever you go, there you are.

JON KABAT-ZINN

When I started working in tech, I was so excited to be in a role and on a team that aligned with my passion and expertise. As more work was assigned to me, I noticed I would mentally take that work home with me. I could be washing dishes, folding clothes, or lying down, and a solution to a problem would come to me. Other times, it would be a follow-up question to something that was said in a meeting. To keep myself from forgetting, I would run to my desk and write it down. Work mentally consumed me.

The interesting thing is, I wasn't unfamiliar with this feeling. I first experienced it when I was building a startup. I loved the people I worked with and the projects I worked on. For the first time in my life, I was able to be my authentic self without corporate consequences. My team encouraged sending memes as a form of communication or using African American Vernacular English to explain ideas. It was beautiful.

What wasn't so beautiful was the lack of work-life balance. It was a beautiful Saturday in the Bay Area, so the girls and I went to the pool. We were laughing and kikiing when I heard an all too familiar sound: "Dun. Dun. Dun. Dun." A Slack message popped up on my computer. (Girl, yes. I brought my laptop to the pool on a Saturday. "We listen and don't judge.") I immediately hopped out of the pool to see what my co-founder had sent me. It was a question about launch day. I sat on a pool chair and started drafting a reply.

My homegirl screamed, "Seriously? Put that laptop away! It's the weekend, and you can do it on Monday."

I looked up at her in confusion and continued typing away.

Because I'd learned that you don't get to take breaks as an entrepreneur—especially when you don't have a profitable business. Success was dependent on how many hours you were willing to put into your dreams. (Think about every billionaire's story about spending all their time in a basement, garage, or dark room to make their product or service profitable.) That meant being available to deal with financial reviews, technical support, marketing, sales, and operations at all times. Right? Because success was all about grit and availability. Right?

Wrong.

A healthy business starts with a healthy being: you. This looks like setting appropriate boundaries with others, but more importantly, yourself. You can say no. And you should. Often. Your passion for the business, project, or team does not make you responsible for saving them. Nor should you tie the success of these things to your availability. There is a way to love what you do and to do it between hours that work in your favor, mentally and physically.

I thought I'd learned the lesson from my startup days, but apparently I hadn't. I was in a new environment, so anxiety was dressed differently and unrecognizable for months. Over time, I picked up the patterns: worry, fear, procrastination, repeat.

So, when I noticed I was anxious and burned out at a new job, for the second time, I knew I needed to take a step back. My manager suggested I take a couple days off.

I headed to my favorite coffee shop with my new book, *Wherever You Go, There You Are*, by Jon Kabat-Zinn. It's a book about meditation: what it is, how we do it, and how we live abundantly because of it.

I desperately wanted to learn how to "get out of my mind and into my body," as my best friend would say. I wanted to learn how to slow down and be present. When I was at work, I was at work. When I was at home, I was at home. I didn't want those lines to be blurred.

As I sat down at my go-to table, I noticed my mind was constantly stuck in the future. Rarely was I present in my surroundings. This kept me in an anxious state, or what I like to call a functioning anxious state. I could move through the world, but I was always concerned with fears of the future or pain from the past. I would ruminate and then anxiously plan how to make sure a negative situation never happened again. I would think,

Miss mamas. You were wildin'! Let's never do that again. 'Kay?

Facts! But what does that mean? How do we make that happen?

Well, let's write down exactly what happened; a play by play of the events and my emotions. Then let's talk about it with our best friend so we can pinpoint the exact moment we went wrong. That way we'll have a record of all the scenarios to look out for.

Beeeeeet! Now you are talking! I love a girl with a plan! It's givinnng self-aware! It's givinnng Program Manager. It's givinnng Doctor of Psychology!

On the outside looking in, I was spiraling. But internally, I was taking control of my life. I thought anxiously planning for the knowns and unknowns of life would bring me the assurance, security, and rest I needed. It didn't. And how could it? Life can't be controlled. It can only be experienced. And, naively, I was trying to control my experience by outthinking it. I thought, *If I have the backup plan for the backup plan, how could I be caught slipping again? Exactly! I couldn't.*

(Insert a visual of me saying this right before my double plan backfires.)

That wasn't the answer. **Wherever you go, there you are** was.

I wasn't ready for what this book, and this affirmation in particular, gave me. It taught me to practice awareness and appreciate stillness. To truly imagine that I am where I am instead of where my mind thinks I am. It taught me how to focus on the reality of what is instead of dwelling on what will be. This meant bringing awareness to my current surroundings. If I am sitting in a crowded room and taking inventory of my thoughts, what am I thinking about? Is it the past, the future, or something that just occurred? Is it a real-time observation? Or is it a judgment, fear, or daydream? If my thoughts do not reflect what I am currently observing, at this exact moment, then I am not present. I am not where I am.

By appreciating the moment we are in, we allow the weight of our lives to come alive. For me, and on that day, it was reminding myself of my environment. "I'm up at my favorite time of the day. I'm in my favorite coffee shop. I'm living in my favorite city in California. I'm drinking the best matcha in the town. They are playing all my favorite songs. I appreciate the outfit choice this guy has made—putting us *all* to shame. I love the smell of those pancakes. I am breathing. I am alive. I am here."

When you bring awareness to your environment, you consciously invite your mind, body, and soul to be present too. You invite them to connect and get on the same page. Together, they work to inform your nervous system that 1. You are okay and 2. Despite your worries, you have permission, and the ability, to return to the safest place you know—you; wherever you are.

Affirmation: Wherever you go, there you are.

Application: Draw back to this affirmation when you feel anxious. Use it to remain rooted in the fact that you are okay because you are here. You are alive and you are breathing. This moment is your moment, regardless of what is going on around you. Let the worries of yesterday and tomorrow stay there. No one can take the present moment from you, so use it to update yourself on what is actually happening—in your environment, not in your head. Be willing to be surprised. Be willing to be where you are.

Exploration:
1. When you take inventory of your thoughts, what's on your mind?
2. Is this happening in the present, past, or future?
   a. If it is not happening right now, write it down so you can release the emotions attached to the event.

b. If it is real-time, what other things are happening in your surroundings? Can you see yourself in this moment (as though you are looking at yourself from outside of yourself)?

3. What emotions does this bring up for you? Gratitude, appreciation, fear?

4. Why?

* * *

You are a spiritual being having a human experience.

PIERRE TEILHARD DE CHARDIN

What do you do when you are doing all the right things to take care of yourself, but you still feel burnt out? You listened to the health gurus, social media influencers, and doctors about the perfect morning and evening routine to live a balanced life, but inside, you feel chaotic. You are going to therapy, journaling, exercising, and even bought an emotional support animal (Ok, maybe this was just me. Let's carry on.), but you still feel disconnected from your faith, purpose, and self.

In 2022 I was doing all the right things to support my mental and physical health, yet I still felt so disconnected. This surprised me because I'd had a similar routine in the pandemic, but the results were different. Back then, I would meditate in the morning, study in the afternoon, and do a walking meditation to finish my day. This routine was my holy grail. While my morning meditation gave me new ideas for my startup, my evening meditation gave me so many ah-has about my behavior, my trauma, and my emotions. I felt complete during a time where there was so much uncertainty.

However, I just couldn't get that enlightenment back, so I brought it up with my therapist. As I explained my level of exhaustion and confusion, she humbly said,

"Yeah, because you are a spiritual being having a human experience."

Now, I'll admit that when she first said it, I was like, "Que?" I was completely lost. She explained that it is a common phrase used to debunk the idea that we need to do something to *feel* connected, versus knowing we already *are* connected. And we experience that connection with God, the Universe, or our Source when we Just. Sit. Still. (Go ahead and pick your jaw up off the floor. Grab mine while you're at it!)

I don't know how she kept pulling out all this wisdom to fit my situation every time, but at that point, I started to think she was ordained and sent to me personally from God.

As we dove deeper, we talked about the difference between the human and spiritual experience. One is rooted in how we perceive and interact with the world around us. The other is how we perceive and interact with the being within us—the Holy Spirit. We don't need to fit peace into our everyday lives because we already have it inside of us. How we access peace depends on our ability to define and organize everyday activities that activate our spiritual connection, or oneness.

My therapist ended our session with homework. That was very on-brand for her. Since my self-care practices weren't working as they used to, she asked me to create a Self-Care Pyramid that outlined activities I would do when I was busy, somewhat busy, and free.

The **Busy** section was at the top of the pyramid. It was an activity that, if done by itself, left me fulfilled, hopeful, and aligned. It didn't need to be paired with anything else to leave me feeling connected to my higher power or self.

The **Somewhat Busy** section was in the middle. These were activities I would do when I had prior work or personal commitments. I could throw in that activity to give myself a boost for the day or week.

The **Free** section was at the bottom of the pyramid. Those were activities that brought me joy but required more of my time and energy.

How to do it:

1. List all your self-care activities on a sheet of paper.
2. To that list, add all the activities that make you happy.
3. Draw a large triangle and divide it into three sections. From top to bottom, label each section *Busy, Somewhat Busy, and Free.*
4. From top to bottom, add two or three activities from your list to each section of your Self-Care Pyramid. You want to use the key activities that impact you most.

- **Helpful:** Think about your responsibilities. Think about the busiest week you've had. What gave you a moment of relief? Was it low effort, high reward? Add that to the top. In the next section, consider whether it required some effort but had a big impact on your mental health. Add it. In the last section, you will have activities that just bring you joy regardless of effort or time.

How it looks:

- **Busy:** one-mile run, call best friend, go to bed early, go to a coffee shop or bookstore, candlelit prayer, hot yoga, walking meditation, solo outing, lie in the sun, journal, or attend church online

- **Somewhat Busy:** visit beach, hang out with best friends, binge Netflix Series, read a book, book a massage, or attend church or life group in person

- **Free:** long workout, bath, vacation, or attend last-minute events with friends.

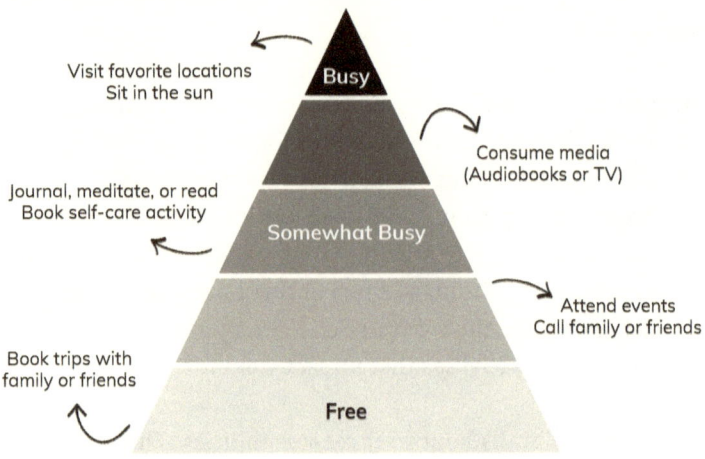

Visit favorite locations
Sit in the sun

Busy

Consume media
(Audiobooks or TV)

Journal, meditate, or read
Book self-care activity

Somewhat Busy

Attend events
Call family or friends

Book trips with
family or friends

Free

Figure 1: Self-Care Pyramid

This exercise helped me navigate the needs of everyday life according to my time and capacity. Doing everything at once did not help me feel connected or rejuvenated. If anything, the endless self-care routines drained me. It was performative, and unfortunately, there was only one person watching it: me. Identifying the impactful activities that I already did and grouping them according to effort and time changed things for me. It kept my spiritual connection flowing amongst my human experiences, such as work, chores, building relationships, and breathing. (I'm only half kidding about breathing.)

I learned that being active in life does not mean you are doing life well. It does not mean that *you* are doing well. Oftentimes, slowing down brings greater results. You can't hear yourself, or Him, if you're on the go. Find the activities that allow you to hear, as well as be present, regardless of the demands of life. After all, you are a spiritual being having a human experience.

Affirmation: You are a spiritual being having a human experience.

Application: Draw back to this affirmation when you are doing everything you can to feel like yourself, but nothing is working. Use it to remain rooted in the fact that the peace you seek is already within you. The teacher appears when the student is ready. So, get ready.

Exploration:
1. What are you currently doing to ensure you feel more like yourself?
2. Do you have a self-care routine? Does it make you feel at home or like a robot?
3. What is the one thing you do to slow down when your schedule or life gets crazy?
4. What's another thing? Make a list. Put it in a Self-Care Pyramid.
5. Collectively, do these activities feel good to you?
6. Do they feel doable based on the effort you can give right now?
   a. If so, act.
   b. If not, get honest with yourself about activities that fuel your inner child.

How Do I Overcome Anxiety?

Anxiety happens when we are trying to plan for all possible outcomes. It's a reminder that we fear things not going the way we planned. It means we are unconsciously looking for something to control, either for our safety or for our comfort.

Anxiety should be acknowledged, thanked, and informed. There is a threshold your body tries to stay within, and when life deviates across it, your nervous system goes into overdrive to keep you "safe." Acknowledge what your anxiety is doing for you. It's planning multiple controlled scenarios for you to feel safe again. However, your body doesn't know how hard it is working to keep you safe. Acknowledge the effort. Thank your body for being so diligent in putting you first. Then, inform your body that you are safe.

Start by slowing down and taking a deep breath. Draw attention to your environment to help you get out of your mind and into your body. This will help bring awareness to the present and not the past or future. Resetting will remind your body that you are okay.

Balancing anxiety is an intentional practice. You have to create environments that support multiple senses at the same time, and sometimes you need additional help to reset your nervous system. That's okay. You will get through it.

You're just a girl. You don't have to solve all the world's problems, or even your own problems, on your own. Lean on your community. Use your resources.

(Now, hold my hand.)

You are worth a slow-burn love and life. Take your time.

four

OVERCOMING CONTROL

when you feel you can't let go—of the outcome or them

Society says you are in control of your life. But that's not always true. Relationships, careers, health, and finances can be unpredictable. Not every unknown or possibility can be planned, controlled, or prevented. As you learned, anxiety doesn't help you plan for your future; it just anxiously tries to control what you can't.

Planning every microdetail of an event won't stop mishaps from happening. Overcommunicating your disdain for lateness won't make people show up on time. Overcommitting at work—even when you are burnt out—won't result in a promotion. And saying yes to your friends every time they invite you to hang out won't make them love or consider you more. In short, people-pleasing will never yield the results you're seeking.

I learned that if I wanted peace, I had to surrender what I thought my life should be like *by now*. To get there, I had to stop putting parameters on the unknowns and trying to control the unexpected. Because it wasn't helping me experience the life of my dreams. If anything, it left me feeling stressed and alienated.

When you feel that you can't let go—of the outcome or them—lean on these affirmations to remind you that you gain control when you release control.

* * *

You're surprised, but God's not surprised.

THERAPIST

Has something ever happened in your life that you would never have imagined? I'm talking about a long-term relationship ending out of nowhere, a friend talking to you crazy, an employer laying you off during the holidays, your co-founder telling you they want to exit the business, or the health issue that the doctors had confirmed was in remission. Things you would never put on your annual bingo card, yet they just happened. Usually, despite your best efforts to manage the foreseen and unforeseen downfall.

I've had many of these moments throughout my life. But the experience that left me in complete shock was when the dynamics with my best friend, David, changed. What shook my core was the relationship ending.

David and I became friends by association. At the time, I was in an on-again-off-again relationship with Aaron. He was looking to save some coins on housing, so he found two guys to get a place with, and boom—his new roommates were now my new friends.

Now, the relationship with David didn't start off with roses and butterflies. The first time we met, we argued in a Chipotle for two hours about the validity of Jesus Christ and Christianity. Things weren't going well. We were two opinionated twenty-somethings talking about the most controversial topic in history. But we became closer when we took a trip to Sol Blume, an R&B music festival in Sacramento, CA.

Over the course of three days, we realized we were more alike than we'd originally thought. We'd both grown up in poverty (truly humble beginnings). And our experiences, wanted and unwanted, had shaped how we showed up in the world. We discovered that a lot of our opinions came from experiencing the woes of life. It was refreshing to turn a new page.

Now, the arguing didn't stop. If anything, we argued more intently because we were family now. ("In the club, we all fam!") From birthdays and road trips to vacations, happy hours, and rap battles, we experienced it all together. 2017–2019 was a time for the ages.

The year 2019 was also the time David and I started going to therapy. This changed our relationship again. Once we had more awareness of our trauma, emotions, and coping mechanisms, we were able to show up for each other in a way that was less combative and more supportive. We knew how to express disap-pointment and pain calmly and with curiosity. Our egos stepped aside so two souls who genuinely wanted the best for each other could step up.

For the next four years, we didn't have another argument. Instead, our relationship became the standard for how I wanted to interact with men in my life. It was a relationship where we could yap about everything under the sun without judgment. One where we didn't have to perform for each other's love and attention. They were given freely because we were invested in each other's well-being. But more importantly, it was an intentional relationship in which time and effort were reciprocated.

It was beautiful—rare, even. It was like having your favorite cousin that you only get to see at family cookouts around all the time. Ready to ride through whatever and for whatever.

The trauma of men? Yeah, it was David cautioning me, "Watch out for him," "Don't do that again. Fix your relationship," or "Stop twerking in the club." (Whoopsy!) At the same time, David was the one asking me introspective questions: "Why do you feel the need to keep responding? What's driving the need to connect after they hurt you?"

Our relationship made me grow. And if I'm honest, it allowed me to heal my relational wounds with men in a safe space. And for that, I was grateful to grow alongside him. I was grateful to be his best friend and big cousin.

I thought nothing could change that. Until something did.

In 2023, he moved across the country to Washington, DC. I was happy for him. Seeing him finally choose himself in a loud way was inspiring. His move would make us—for the first time—long-distance friends. But I didn't think anything of it. Out of all my friends, I knew our relationship could withstand change.

Girl, it didn't. Within six months, I noticed the old dynamic we'd worked so hard to keep out started to creep back in. Intentionality, communication, emotional awareness, and physical availability started to fade. The things our relationship thrived on were no longer there. And it became emotional labor trying to add those elements back in. I watched my healthiest relationship turn into one that needed excessive effort to maintain.

I was shocked, and honestly, completely gutted. How could the standard turn into the bare minimum? How could the strong foundation turn into quicksand? Was Mars in retrograde? Not that I believed in the stars, but I was trying to apply any reasoning to give me *a* reason. I took the wait-it-out approach, thinking maybe the change was temporary and I was just making a big deal out of nothing. *He is getting his footing in a new city, a new role, and new relationships. It's not forever; it's just right now.*

As the months went by, the relationship became more strained. David and I struggled to figure out the change.

Girl, I ran—not walked—to my therapist, Amina. I opened up the Zoom call and explained what I was observing. Then, with tears in my eyes and overwhelm in my voice, I said, "I'm just surprised that this is even happening. If this was anyone else, I would accept it and move on. But this relationship? I'm shocked. I'm hurt."

In an attempt to help me sort out my life, she humbly reminded me,

"You're surprised, but God's not surprised."

Meaning nothing happened that He didn't already know could and would happen. My first thought was, *Why would she say the perfect thing at the perfect time so that I would perfectly cry like that?* My second thought was, *She is right.*

I was surprised because I wasn't expecting it, and despite my best efforts, I couldn't control the relationship dynamic. Really, I couldn't control him. I couldn't choose how he supported me. I only had his assurance that I was heard and his promise of changed behavior.

In 2024, I moved to Washington, DC. Our relationship was still weird, but I thought everything would change once we were face-to-face. I reassured myself that my concerns would subside and we would go back to our normal dynamic once we were in the same place, like old times.

Well, no. The tension grew. That led to us avoiding the hard conversations and eventually each other for the sake of peace. When we finally were able to discuss everything, we spent six hours outside a museum, talking in circles. I couldn't understand where the tension was coming from, and the more he explained, the more we were confused. It was hard, but it made me realize something very honest.

We experienced so much change in 2024 that, naturally, we changed too. How we moved through the world then was not how we'd moved in 2022 or 2019. We grew, and unfortunately, that growth took us in different directions. But we didn't want to let go. The friction came because we weren't ready to accept that what we needed in a friend no longer existed in the other person. The year we were supposed to repair our relationship turned into the year we ended it.

I spent the following year (yes, year) journaling through the pain. I was all talked out over something that wasn't going to change, but my heart was still heavy, so I wrote what I could to process my emotions and adjust to my new normal. Whenever the moment got too heavy—for me and the page—I recalled "You're surprised, but God's not surprised." Every time I found myself ruminating on what had or hadn't happened, I would go back and reread those words in my journal. They brought me comfort and clarity when I didn't have any.

And I hope they bring the same to you.

Life has many unexpected turns, but God already knows what will happen next. So, while you may be shocked, He is not. Not only is He not shocked, but He has already ordained the next steps for you. You just have to have enough awareness to notice the moment for what it is—*a moment*. Then choose your reaction and decision.

Those I-cannot-believe-this-is-happening moments are stepping stones to the next stage of your life. They give you the skills to handle the seasons you are about to walk into. In every season you lose something—a relationship, job, or valuable item—you gain something. Sometimes, the same day. Remember that. You are not living a life of punishment. You are living life as a witness. A witness to love, joy, loss, and grief. No experience is left out. So, take it in. Experience it. Don't try to control it.

I couldn't control that ending, but that affirmation taught me I didn't have to. It was our time. A year later, we finally talked it out. While the pain was still there, there wasn't any beef for my favorite human. It was just love for an era that we'd had. One I'll cherish forever. Knowing that I could always return to memories, lessons, and laughs brought me peace.

Release what you can't let go of, so what you need can find you.

Affirmation: You're surprised, but God's not surprised.

Application: Draw back to this affirmation whenever things happen that are outside of your control. Use it to remain rooted in the fact that, regardless of what is happening right now, it will all be okay. Open up your heart to the possibility that life is changing, and so are you. Be open to being surprised and being *the* surprise. Because you are the example that proves that miracles do happen. God is still working in your favor, even when you can't see it. Whatever you are going through is already getting better.

Exploration:
1. What big moments in your life are you surprised about?
2. Did you see it coming?
3. How can you give yourself space to feel your emotion and grace to release the emotion?
4. What skills are you learning or unlearning as you navigate this transition?
5. What I-can-not-believe-this-is-happening moment or experience do you want to have for your praise report or your prayer report?

* * *

Let go or be dragged.

THERAPIST

Have you ever wanted something so bad that you were willing to put aside all logic for it? Your friends told you to look closer at the red flags, but you felt they just didn't know the whole story. You thought that if they felt the butterflies and excitement that you did, then they would see it your way. They would put aside their opinions and support you. But they didn't. So, you trusted your gut, ignored their advice, and moved forward with the job, relationship, or business. You were confident that you had everything under control. Hell, you might have been positive that it was a gift from God. Until He showed you otherwise.

In December 2023, I decided to move across the country. I was packing up everything I owned in Oakland, CA, and moving to Washington, DC. I had a lot to do between selling furniture, hiring movers, and seeing all the friends I'd made over the past eight years. My mental capacity was at an all-time low.

To sort out the madness, I spent the majority of my last days at Kinfolx. It was a new coffee shop that was open all day, serving coffee in the morning and wine at night. It became the go-to spot for coworking, networking, and lounging. And I never missed a Friday there.

By April, I was mostly done with planning. The big-ticket items were done, but I needed to tie up some small details. I got dressed in my business casual attire and walked over to Kinfolx.

When I opened the double doors, I immediately heard Frank Ocean over the speakers. I smiled and thought, *Now, these are my people!* I took a few more steps in and was greeted with a line. Kinfolx always had a line at their counter. And I was always going to jump into it. Coins ready. Purse open. Rehearsing my go-to order: one oxtail patty with a matcha latte.

As I waited my turn, I looked around for seating. My eyes scanned the burnt orange chairs, communal table, and window seating. I saw a spot open by the window. I was about to run over to reserve it when I heard, "What do you normally get here?"

I turned around to face the deep voice behind me. I looked up and saw a tall, caramel-toned man looking me intently in my eyes. (Ah!) My first thought was, *There is a God!* My second was, *Is he talking to me? Girl, say something back!*

I did my best to respond in a calm tone. "I normally get a Jamaican patty with a matcha."

"Oh, is it good? I don't normally drink matcha. I usually get an espresso."

"Oh, I love it! I get it all the time. It's chef's kiss," I said enthusiastically.

He smiled.

I turned back around to avoid awkwardly staring him into his soul. (I'm only partially kidding.) I remembered my spot by the window. By that time, multiple spots had opened up.

Then I heard, "You want to share a table?" (Not to sound delusional, but that was basically a marriage proposal. Right?) I nodded yes. I was still too stunned to speak. Drew and I exchanged stories for over two hours. He was kind, funny, and overall intriguing. At the end of the conversation, we said our goodbyes.

A few weeks later, we randomly saw each other again at Kinfolx. This was our third encounter, and we had already exchanged numbers to share resources about jobs we discussed. During this particular encounter, he offered to give me a ride home since he'd seen that I was always walking. That ride home led to us going to a nearby restaurant and yapping for hours in the sun. We talked about family dynamics, fears, short-term goals, and our faith journeys. It was so wholesome and fun.

One of the things that stood out to me was how vulnerable he was. Even in our first conversation, I knew things about him that I probably shouldn't—like how he was struggling with job loss and the idea of moving back home as an adult. I empathized because I was no stranger to life transitions. I appreciated our conversations and making a friend who was well-travelled, honest, and had emotional depth. I remember thinking, *God, when I said I wanted to meet a nice man, I didn't mean in Oakland. I didn't mean right before I'd have to leave.*

Over the next few months, we would run into each other around town or at Kinfolx. Same electric vibe, but add in a bit more sexual tension. One night, as we were leaving a day party, I decided to address the elephant in the room.

"What's going on? How do you feel? I'm getting mixed vibes from you," I texted.

My phone rang. It was Drew.

"Hey, I got your message. And I like you. I think you're attractive, too. But I'm hesitant due to my financial situation," he replied.

He hadn't expected the job hunt to last so long, and it was taking a toll on him. I let him know I appreciated his telling me how he felt. It was mutual, and I extended grace to him.

We continued to get to know each other. However, over time, I started noticing things that made me raise an eyebrow: his hesitation to hang out after a certain time of night, his desire to bring his homeboy when I invited him personally to events, or his inability to follow through on hangout sessions he had brought up. Add in a few more red flags, and I was deep in a therapy session, trying to understand the ways of a man. (Yuck!)

My therapist, Amina, was a poised woman. She always let me talk uninterrupted before she lifted her notebook to show me diagrams of proven clinical theories and ways the things I said were tied back to the diagram, my needs, or my future self. That moment wasn't any different. She listened to me connect the dots on my own theories before she said graciously,

"Yeah, you get to decide if you want to let go or be dragged."

Now, cut the cameras! Why would she say that? In front of everybody! (Girl, it was just me, but I was embarrassed for both of us.)

She explained I had two options: I could take the concerning data I had and let go of the relationship, or continue the relationship and get dragged in the process.

I had to sit with that. Do I let go of the possibility of something new because of a few things I can't control, or do I wait it out and see what God has in store for me? Do I block him on my phone and choose another coffee shop, or let the chips fall where they may—*even* if it's to the pits of hell? (Yes, my decision-making is dramatic—like me.)

Unfortunately, I chose the drag-me-through-the-mud route. Cringe? I know! I kind of wish Amina had labeled it as the-biggest-mistake-in-your-life so I could've given the option the severity it deserved.

That same week, I told my girlfriends how I was feeling. They had tough questions for me. "Do you think he has a girlfriend?" they asked in a curious but already-solved-the-case kind of way.

"No!" I quickly assured them.

Although it was a thought, I knew it wasn't possible. He had been vulnerable and honest about a lot since day one. If that was the case, he would have mentioned it. In our very first conversation, Drew assured me that he didn't have a partner.

When my last month in Oakland came, I threw a party with my closest friends and invited him. I wanted my closest friends to form their own opinion outside of what I had shared. After the event, all my girls said we looked great together, and they could tell I was happy. (Yay me!) That made me blush. Then they shared that he also gave "fuck boy" vibes. (Welp . . .)

They said what I feared, and silently thought, out loud. I asked myself, *Are you going to listen to their feedback? I mean, you spent many years not listening to their concerns about your romantic partners. And you can't say it ever worked out in your favor. So, it might be time to do things a little differently. These are your very best friends expressing concern early on. You trust their counsel in every area of your life. So, why disregard their opinion in this area now?*

I decided I wouldn't do that again. If my friends saw something I didn't while in the "honeymoon stage," then I wanted to extend gratitude for those second, third, and fourth sets of eyes. I didn't share my personal feelings or life with many, but my friends safeguarded my emotions, time after time.

In the days that followed, I expressed my hesitations and desires to pull back. In those conversations, Drew asked for more of my time and presence. Blatantly, he asked me to "stay." I obliged. I thought maybe this was a lesson in patience or a blessing in disguise. I wanted to let time reveal the truth.

When I moved to the East Coast in June 2024, I found out within thirty days that Drew was already in a long-term, cross-country relationship. Unfortunately, I didn't find out from him.

Girl, I got dragged. And as hard as it was to sit with, it was the path I had chosen. I chose to see it through instead of ending things when the red flags presented themselves. As I sent my last message to Drew—letting him know that he'd played the wrong one—I couldn't help but envision Tyra Banks on *America's Next Top Model* screaming at me, "Learn something from this!" When the red flags were confirmed, I wanted to give grace. "Learn something from this!" Finally, I did.

How often do we stick around for the plot? We stick around to confirm or deny our assumptions about people. We stick around because we so desperately want to be wrong and have the ending of our desires. Not realizing that sticking around is hurting us. Not realizing that playing the wait-and-see game is willingly signing up to be emotionally dragged.

This is true in relationships, but it's also true in our careers. We apply for roles, go through multiple interviews, and wait months for a rejection email or call. We knew something was off when the recruiter stopped initiating feedback. We knew something was off when the interviewer changed the interview time last minute. We knew something was off when the start date got pushed out. But we wait to see.

If you are presented with data that is concerning your spirit, listen to it. The logic you put aside for your own desires? Pick it back up, girlfriend. It's time to state the obvious, or, as my grandma would say, call a spade a spade. If it's not a yes, then it's a no. If it's not a definitive yes ("You got the job," "I want to marry you," or "I want you to join the team"), then it's a no. And when you hear the "no" directly or intertwined with confusion, do the hard thing and let go before you're left picking up the pieces from being dragged.

You deserve definitive answers, not empty promises. And if someone else can't provide them to you, you have the power to give them to yourself. But you can only get to this level of empowerment when you release control. When you release the desire to wait and see what another person is going to do, especially after they've already shown you how they will handle you, you gain control. You get to decide whether you want your life to stay the way it is or move in a different direction.

Choose wisely.

Affirmation: Let go or be dragged.

Application: Draw back to this affirmation when you are looking for reasons to stay when the data is telling you to leave. Use it to remain rooted in the fact that you already have the answer you are asking God to provide. You already have the community to help you see what you are intentionally trying to avoid. Lean into them. Lean into releasing control of the outcome because it might not get you your desired result. Trust what you hear, see, and know.

Exploration:
1. What are you holding onto against the advice of your friends, family, or medical team?
2. Why is this situation or relationship important to you?
3. What needs are being met as a result of maintaining this relationship?
   a. Is there another avenue for your needs to be met that supports you and is supported by your community? By no means should you live your life for others, but you should take note of the counsel from your peers and family. Not to dictate your life, but to inform your decisions.
4. What would happen if you let it continue?
5. What would happen if you let it go?
6. Which path do you genuinely prefer? Decide.

* * *

Your new life is going to cost you your old one.

BRIANNA WIEST

Whenever I wanted something new, such as an outfit, meal, or extended vacation, I would have to make a trade-off. I would say, *If you get this, then you can't get that. So, which one do you really want? Okay, now put everything else back because you're acting like money grows on trees!* Reluctantly, I had to release something in order to gain something. Yet I never thought this would apply to my life.

The Bay Area was my home for eight years. I experienced hiking, rafting, skiing, and so many other first-time adventures while on the West Coast. While I knew it wasn't my forever home, I didn't have a real reason to leave—until I did.

My last year in California was riddled with fear, uncertainty, and anxiety. After a TikTok went viral teaching viewers how to steal Kia and Hyundai cars, every major city across the United States started getting run through by the "Kia Boys." Unfortunately for me, Oakland was a hotspot.

Three days after moving into a new apartment with secure parking, my car was stolen. It's hard to describe what being a victim of theft feels like. I was just at a loss for words. Partially because— who does that? But mostly because my car held sentimental value: it was the last thing my late grandpa picked out for me. I never planned to part with that car, yet it was taken without being asked. That made me mad as hell. Overnight, my means of transport, and my connection to someone special, were gone. I had to make new plans.

Since I was in no rush to make car payments or get robbed again, I decided to walk and Uber everywhere for the summer. I thought that would give me a much-needed mental break. It didn't. My daily walks consisted of watching presumably regular cars pull up and break into unattended cars. It became so bad that most people just left their windows down to avoid paying deductible fees every few months. It was that frequent.

I became scared. When cars crept up next to my Uber or rental car, I feared I was about to become the next victim of a robbery. It felt crazy to think like that, but I saw it happen consistently in broad daylight. Most times, in front of the police station. I consistently watched the police do nothing. After a few months, victims started getting hurt when they tried to fight back. That left me even more scared. But I couldn't stay car-less forever.

So, after four months of walking, I mustered up the courage to get a new car. Within fifteen days, I walked out of the bank to find masked men checking my new car for valuables—as I was walking up to it! Girl, it was 8:00 a.m., raining, and a Tuesday. I thought to myself, *If you can't go to Bella Noche on a Tuesday, then where the hell can you go?* (I'm only slightly kidding.) But that was the final straw. I felt no time or place was safe. I became scared—All. The. Time.

I knew I needed to think seriously about other cities I could move to. I worked remotely, was single, and didn't have anything keeping me in Oakland except my community. But in 2023, that started to shift as well. Many of my close friends moved out of state, and the ones that were local turned into "let's set up a call to catch up next month" friends—even though they lived less than thirty minutes from me. I felt disconnected and alone even when I wasn't alone. I was also riddled with fear and anxiety, so I desperately wanted to cling to the safety of my community. But I couldn't. All at once,

I felt as though my life of safety, community, and peace was coming to an end.

In September 2023, I started planning my new life. I knew I wanted to do a few things:

1. Move out of California.
2. Feel safe again.
3. Stop begging my close friends to show up for me when I need them.
4. Bonus: Join the majority race, not the minority race, in my new city.

By December, I had decided Washington, DC, was the place where I'd start again.

I started by sending a mass message to everyone I'd met in the Bay. I told them I was leaving in six months and throwing a going-away party that they were all invited to. The acceptances came rolling in. At the same time, I spoke with my manager about my desire to move out of state. I was prepared for whatever he would say about my future with the company. Thankfully, he supported my decision and made my role remote indefinitely.

The only thing left was to spend time with my favorite people doing my favorite things: hiking new trails, visiting Kinfolx, eating at my Burmese-Ethiopian-Thai rotation, and catching sunsets on the coast. When the party came, we danced all night. Then my friends gave me an hour of testimonies about how I had impacted their lives and defined what community meant to them. I didn't expect that. For the first time in a long time, I felt loved by my peers. I already knew I was, but it was hard to feel love when fear was my dominant emotion.

When I finally got to Washington, DC, I had the opportunity to build a new life. I already had a starter list of what I wanted. I just needed to go and get it. Before I moved over, I followed social media pages that were specific to DC. This gave me an idea of events happening in the area and groups I could join, such as a running club or tennis club. Through one of those pages, I made my first friend. Once I arrived, we met up, and she introduced me to another one of her friends. My community was growing, and I was only three days into being a DC resident of Chocolate City, another name for the area due to its high population of Black residents. Unexpectedly, my new life was meeting all my needs.

I was even starting to feel safe again. On my first day, I went to Target and saw that no one was worried about the stuff in their cars. No one was hiding their chargers, backpacks, or shopping bags to prevent their quarter windows from being broken into. I was shocked! After a few more errands, I felt crazy obsessing over my safety. I finally saw how unnatural and uncommon living with fear and anxiety was. Having consistent evidence that I was safe reset my nervous system. I can't tell you how refreshing it was to finally breathe again. I could leave my house without stopping to look over my shoulder and just exist in the world. It was almost as if I went back in time to a headspace where I was unjaded and naive. Finally, my nervous system was at peace.

As I reflected on my life, I sat in awe. God had really done His big one on me, and I was so grateful. Everything on my prayer list He had provided: community, safety, belonging. Well, almost everything.

You remember when I said I didn't want to beg my friends to show up when I needed them? Yeah, I thought it would look like deeper conversations and understanding with my current friends, as well as meeting people who naturally aligned with the current version of myself. Yeah, no. What that actually meant was that God was going to remove every person that I was begging, even if they were my best friend. (Jump scare.)

In three to six months, I parted ways with three of my best friends. (Yup, the same ones you've seen me cry about in these pages.) Relationships that had shaped me, grown me, and taught me the meaning of platonic love ended. Over the course of multiple, hour-long conversations, one thing became apparent. While the love was strong, the pressure to be who we used to be was too high. We no longer were those younger versions of ourselves, and trying to maintain those images, at our big age, wasn't sustainable. At that time, we couldn't be what the other needed and wanted. It gutted me.

I remember saying, "One relationship? Okay. I don't want to accept it, but I'll trust You. But three? God please! Make it make sense."

I was beyond depressed. For months, I questioned God and turned my back on relationships. I thought that after everything I'd learned, practiced, and communicated about my feelings, desires, and pains to my friends, I would never have difficulty with relationships again. I was wrong. It was that same assumption that blinded me from seeing that the people I was begging to show up weren't some random girls I'd met over the weekend but my best friends. On many occasions, in different ways. And usually after spending hours communicating what we wanted from the relationship.

I learned that sometimes love and history aren't enough. When my relationships felt as though they were on the brink, I needed to step back and look at the situation more objectively. If I was asking for the same thing over and over, but I was not getting it, I had to make a decision. I could decide to stay and *keep* asking or leave and trust God would place me in environments where I didn't have to ask. And as sure as the sun rises, He did.

He is willing to give you everything you desire when you are willing to release everything to Him—even the people you love more than anything.

He gave me my heart's desires when I accepted that my new life was going to cost me my old one. It wasn't an easy or overnight journey. It was slow and painful. I was so excited about my next chapter in life, and more importantly, the safety and peace I would find once I got there, that I didn't know it was going to cost me something to get it. The Bay Area gave me community, job security, and experiences of a lifetime. I wanted that again, but I didn't realize I would have to release control over my current life to get my new life. I thought I would get more blessings on top of my previous blessings. God said, "No. I have to swap them out. They aren't serving you the way I want them to. Give me that so I can give you this." Rooted in my faith, I surrendered to the process.

If you are fighting to keep something in your life, ask yourself, "Is this getting me closer to my dreams? Is this fulfilling my heart's desires?" Answer it truthfully. Don't dwell on whether it met your needs in the past, but ask yourself whether this thing meets your needs *today*. Past blessings are still blessings, but they don't always help you gain new ones. Be willing to see how good a new life can get when you release the old one.

Affirmation: Your new life is going to cost you your old one.

Application: Draw back to this affirmation when you feel you are losing control over your finances, relationships, or even mental health. Use it to remain rooted in the fact that the habits you are putting in place and the decisions you are making for yourself are going to get you the life of your dreams. While it may feel as if everything is falling apart, remember that it is really all coming together. For your good and His glory.

Exploration:
1. What does your current life look like?
2. What do you want it to look like?
3. What is it going to cost you?
4. Are you afraid to lose those things or people? (If you are, good. It means you are human. But remember, all you're going to lose is what was built for a person you no longer are.)
5. What activities can you start to support your new life?
6. Who can support you as you navigate this transition?

* * *

Let it come undone so I can build it to what it's supposed to be.

SARAH JAKES ROBERTS

I don't know whether this is anyone else's testimony, but I'm actually not good with change. Mostly because it's a learned skill. If I spend days, weeks, or months planning my life, I don't want any problems with it going my way. I want everything to line up perfectly. Taking a left instead of a right on my roadmap is not an issue. But getting a whole new roadmap? Oh, girl, I have issues with that. I keep a tight grip on my plans. So if anything—and I do mean anything—changes, I'm thrown into a tizzy. Because it's hard to release my plans or someone else's. And if forced to change, I struggle with asking or receiving help on the new plan.

This was the case when I found out I had Polycystic Ovarian Syndrome, or PCOS. Girl, yes. At thirty-two, I was diagnosed with a chronic, hormonal disorder—despite showing symptoms for six years.

It was a heartbreaking and eye-opening experience. How could I have the best insurance, and regular appointments, and still not receive adequate treatment? How could the signs be there and multiple doctors miss it? Each doctor would test for the same thing, and when the results showed "unremarkable," they would say I was fine. But I wasn't. The symptoms got worse. Year after year. Visit after visit. It seemed everyone was treating a problem and not a person. It seemed they wanted to find a quick fix and not a holistic solution. It seemed as if no one cared about what I was saying or going through. Until someone did.

When I moved to DC, I had to get a new primary doctor. So, I went online and found someone who was covered in my new plan. She was a Black woman who had great reviews and seemed inviting in her profile picture. (It doesn't take much to please me.) I went in for a routine, new patient appointment and came out feeling seen and heard. In the midst of showing her my notes from my previous appointments and going through my family history, she asked questions that no one else had, such as, "When do you experience acne? Where does it usually show up? Do you get velvety patches around your neck? Have you noticed any skin tags?" She dug deeper into the things that other doctors told me were "normal." Came to find out they weren't.

My symptoms and experience had a name—a common one at that— and it was PCOS. A hormonal imbalance that can cause weight gain, hormonal acne along your chin, chronic fatigue, ADHD-type symptoms such as brain fog, facial hair, missed periods, and cysts.

I cried when she told me. Not because she gave me an answer, but because no one else had. I was disappointed. I felt I could no longer trust the medical system. How could I have a team of minority women for six years and not receive adequate, quality, or holistic care? I completely shut down. I left my appointment overwhelmed with information and management options (because there wasn't a cure). I told her I needed time, and she respected my wishes.

Now, I didn't know enough about my diagnosis or what I should do, so I ran to social media for more information. I thought, "What are the girls saying about this? Am I the only one whose life is falling apart?" What I found was community. Not only was I one of many, but there were a bunch of nutritionists focused on PCOS management available.

After my recent experience, I reached out to a Black nutritionist on Instagram. She was promising a four-month program that would change how I looked and felt. I wanted that, but I didn't believe her. With everything going on, I was scared to fall for another program promising results from a plan that worked for them but no one else. So, when she replied, I left her response on read. I didn't have another option, but I couldn't trust the one I had.

In the meantime, I was just trying to make it through the day without ending up on the floor crying. I couldn't finish a single task without forgetting what I was doing. I didn't feel like myself. Really, I didn't feel human. I was experiencing all the stages of grief: denial, anger, bargaining, depression, and sometimes, acceptance.

I didn't know what to do, so I did the only thing I knew how to do: I went to church. I was new to the area, so my homegirl recommended her church. That Sunday, the lead pastor's wife was preaching from Acts 9:10-18. It was the story of Saul and Ananias, a messenger God sent to guide Saul through his situation. Saul, who became the apostle Paul, was blind and asked God to speak to him. He was unaware that God answered his prayers with a person. Instead of speaking directly to Saul, God sent Ananias. Saul was waiting to hear from God without realizing that Ananias was the answer he was waiting on.

Girl, I was sobbing before the sermon finished. Here I was leaving my own Ananias on read instead of taking the help I was desperately pleading for. But my mind had led me to believe that no one could help me. That no matter what the health professionals said, I would never get better. The recommendations, medicine, and assurances were all empty promises. They had failed me. That's what I believed, and no one could change my mind—but God.

The nutritionist was persistent. Once a week, she was in my direct messages, promising to help me. After two weeks, she increased her outreach to every forty-eight hours. (That was a woman who was sure about her abilities. And we love to see it.) After thirty days—after *that* sermon—I hopped on an intro call with Courtney Minors.

Girl, I found my Ananias! Courtney worked with my primary doctor, and together they ordered the necessary tests to build me a holistic wellness plan. Within two weeks, I could complete daily tasks again. Within three weeks, I was losing weight for the first time in three years—and people were noticing! In three months, all my symptoms were gone, my hormone levels were normal, and I'd lost sixteen pounds. My doctors were shocked, and so was I. She did everything she said she was going to do as a provider: provide!

As I reflected on how God came through for me, I remembered a sermon I'd watched by Sarah Jakes Roberts. It was called "The Undoing," and she said,

> **"Let it come undone so I can build it to what it's supposed to be."**

Per usual, I cried. I'd spent so many years doing what I was *supposed* to do. If I complained that I was gaining weight, my doctors would tell me to just work out. If I expressed concerns about my period or hormones, they would tell me to get on birth control. For years, I was hiking, running, cycling, rowing, and doing strength training or Pilates to no avail. The results were not resulting. I had let go of the *traditional* and recommended treatment plans, so new plans could be built. I'd never worked with a nutritionist before and was skeptical whether her methods would make a difference, but they did!

My life changed when I stopped letting *my* way get in *the* way. This meant I had to stop letting the way I used to do things be the only way of doing things. My first mistake was not taking advantage of all the healthcare resources I had at my disposal. My second mistake was thinking my healthcare providers were working to treat my whole self and not just the first issue I presented to them. In the end, those mistakes became valuable lessons.

If you are on a health journey where you have more concerns than answers, here's what you can do:

1. **Keep track of your symptoms.** Journal every time you feel unwell. This allows you to see patterns clearly. For example, you might notice that you get headaches following your workouts. Or you may see that you get a sharp pain in your leg almost every other week. This is data that needs to be shared. What seems insignificant in a single moment can turn out to be a pattern over time. It's important—critical even—to not rely on your memory to carry you 365 days into your *one* routine appointment.

2. **Utilize your resources.** Ask for more, early and often; this includes additional bloodwork and tests. Utilize every benefit you have in your insurance plan. After all, you've already paid for it. If your primary doctor is not knowledgeable in the area you are having issues with, go to a specialist or holistic doctor. There is a medical expert for every ailment you have. Find them and get the answers you need.

3. **Advocate for yourself.** If a doctor's not listening to your concerns or you're not getting what you need, find another one. You have free will. And more importantly, you have a right to comprehensive medical care. Don't feel bad about wanting more answers or consideration. If something is bothering you, get to the bottom of it. Use marketplaces such as ZocDoc to help you find medical professionals who take your insurance. Be active about finding the person who cares about your health as much as you do.

Affirmation: Let it come undone so I can build it to what it's supposed to be.

Application: Draw back to this affirmation when your way is not going to plan but you are not trusting anyone else's either. Use it to remain rooted in the fact that the help you desire is on the other side of your ask. Trust that by opening up about your needs, your Ananias is getting into position to support you. Trust that the teacher appears when the student is ready. Ask yourself if you are ready. Then, take that first step forward.

Exploration:
1. What is one battle that you really need help with?
2. Have you communicated your need for help?
3. Who has offered to help you?
   a. In what ways have they offered help?
4. Even if it's not the way you would do things, are you willing to accept the help?
5. Are you willing to let your way come undone so another way can form?
   a. If you're not, what do you think would happen if you did it a different way?

* * *

LOVE: Letting. Others. Voluntarily. Evolve.

MELISSA HEISLER

Growing up as the eldest daughter left me with a lot of responsibility. Not only was I tasked with setting an example for my siblings, but I was simultaneously pushed to break generational curses, such as obtaining a college degree. The more I reached new heights in my family, the more I was tasked with helping my siblings to do the same. Or, at the very least, talking "sense" into them if they were steering away from my path. It was exhausting. And I didn't realize it until I was discussing family dynamics in therapy. My sister was graduating high school, and I was falling into a role that wasn't mine to play—parent.

In October 2019, I was catching up with my little sister about her senior year. As I lived in California and she lived in Florida with her dad, many of our updates were by phone. I texted her to see when she was free from school and work. She immediately replied with her availability. I gave her a ring later that day.

"Hey sissyyy," I said in my high-pitched voice. "How are you? How is school?"

"School is fine. I had the day off today, so I'm doing some writing," she answered earnestly.

"Oh, okay! We love a little break. Well, you're a senior now. Are you excited about going to college and getting out of your dad's house? A little taste of freedom."

There was a brief silence. She chuckled and said, "No! I don't ever want to leave Baba's house. I want to stay here forever."

I was confused. Wasn't it every kid's dream to get away from the rules and expectations of their parents? What was she talking about? Forever? I pushed my assumptions aside.

"Well, fair. You have a sweet gig of not paying rent. You should probably hold onto that for as long as possible, girl. Trust me," I said. Speaking from experience.

"Yeah." She agreed while letting out a giggle.

"Well, it's October. Have you started applying to colleges?"

"No," she said definitively. "I need to take the SAT first. My guidance counselor signed me up to take it, but I forgot about it when the day came."

"Forgot about it? Lawd. Did you sign up to retake it?"

"Ha-ha, not yet," she said confidently.

As a first-generation student, I knew the October to December timeframe was critical for her getting into college and getting a good financial aid package, so I began to worry about her future.

"Okay. Well, you want to take it sooner than later so you can start applying to colleges. It's better to apply before winter so you can get an early decision," I summarized to avoid sounding too preachy or maternal.

"Okay. I will," she said.

I made another suggestion. "You should also have your dad sign you up for financial aid for next year."

"Okay. They were talking about this at school, but I wasn't paying too much attention. I'll have to look into it. He might have already done it."

"Okay . . ." I said with increasing concern. "Let me know if you need my help with anything!"

I started to pick up that maybe she wasn't as interested in college as I was. She had a routine, and she was good with that. She was happy with how things were. More importantly, she felt safe in her environment. I didn't push the matter any further. I shifted the conversation to her latest hobbies and interests.

As she was talking, I zoned out, thinking about the last conversation I'd had with my great-grandma. She was asking about my siblings and how active I was in their lives. I was eighteen and in my first year of college at the time, so I told her, "Not that active, but I call when I can." She made me promise to make an effort to watch over and care for them. I agreed and brushed it off, not knowing she would go to be with the Lord a month later.

Hearing my sister talk about her future so haphazardly made me nervous. I was concerned that her lack of urgency and planning would make her miss her window of opportunity. I blamed myself for not calling her earlier in the year to prepare her for college. I started to believe I was failing as a big sister.

And I carried that belief for months. I thought attending my biggest achievements was enough to inspire my siblings. And showing them a different life was enough to make them want more for themselves.

It wasn't. Those things impacted me but did nothing for them. It was just a "good for you." I didn't know what else I could do to make a difference in their lives. I didn't know how I could live up to my promise or my big sister title.

I went into my second session with Amina so overwhelmed by responsibilities that I couldn't hold back the tears any longer. I felt as if everyone was looking for me to guide somebody, when I just wanted to guide myself. I just wanted to be responsible for myself. I was still young and didn't know what I was doing with my life, yet I was being told to guide someone else's life. It felt as if my "duty" was unattainable. I cried until my soul sighed.

Amina looked at me with so much love and concern. "You can put the bags down. The responsibility and weight you are carrying for adults in your life are not yours. Your sister has chosen a different path, and that is okay."

"LOVE is Letting Others Voluntarily Evolve."

When I tell you I wept like Jesus wept, I *wept*. I'd never had someone absolve me of familial responsibilities. I didn't know what it was like to not own others' successes and failures.

As the eldest, it is ingrained in us to assume responsibility for our siblings. And somehow their outcomes are a reflection of our influence, and not our parents' teachings. It's a confusing and heavy responsibility.

A prime example for those who have siblings: Remember when we were told to watch our siblings; then they went off and did something wrong. The first thing our parents asked was, "Why did you let them do that? Why weren't you watching them?" As if somehow, we magically joined bodies during their crime spree and split right before our parents came back.

Detaching responsibility from others is hard to learn, especially if we were always placed in positions of control. However, when we let our family and closest friends choose who *they* want to be versus who *we* want them to be, we allow our relationships to grow stronger.

My sister never ended up going to college. Instead, she built a beautiful life where she felt safe and happy in a place outside of her childhood home. She is a lover of animals, storytelling, and people. She moved out of state, found a partner, and is living a life worth living. I'm glad she was able to discover how to shine her own light without the dictation of others. On her own, she became who she was meant to be.

Affirmation: LOVE is Letting. Others. Voluntarily. Evolve.

Application: Draw back to this affirmation when you notice that others are not meeting your expectations. Use it to remain rooted in the fact that we all have free will and your loved ones' decisions may not look like your decisions. That is okay. You can support them anyway. When they want help, they will ask. The more you can sit in silence with them, the more they will lean on you for comfort.

Exploration:
1. What decision is your loved one making that doesn't sit right with you? Why?
2. What would you prefer they do?
    a. Acknowledge these are expectations.
3. Can you support them despite your expectations or desires?

a. If so, can you communicate your desire without holding them hostage to your desired outcome?
b. If so, what environment and tone would be most supportive for this conversation?
c. If not, can you listen to what your loved one needs without providing verbal support?

How Do I Overcome the Need to Control?

You experience the need to control when you are scared of losing something: your dreams, dignity, relationships, or even ideas of what the future is supposed to be. However, if you hold on too tightly to fear and try to control what's already changing, things fall apart even more.

You overcome the need to control by first recognizing its grip. Write down what your actions are intending to achieve. Is it stability, comfort, financial increase, or something else? Then write down the ways it is trying to get you those things. Are you forcing something that's no longer working? Are you ignoring red flags? Are you burning the midnight oil—staying up until you are completely exhausted? Then, be honest with yourself. Is it working? Are you actually in control?

If you find yourself with more questions than answers, remember that gaining control starts by releasing it. It starts when you take the pressure off yourself to make everything right, perfect, or true. Remember, nothing is happening that shouldn't. Trust that you have the data, community, and inner knowing to rise above any challenge you are facing.

While you may be surprised, God's not. In fact, He is showing you that your new life is going to cost you your old one. What are you willing to let go to receive it—ego, anger, control, relationships, negative thoughts, outdated patterns? Because control does not equal safety. It will not get you the desires of your heart.

(Now, hold my hand.)

Only you will. Let it go.

five

OVERCOMING ANGER

when you feel you have been wronged

Anger comes on the tail end of things not going your way or as you had expected. It happens after you realize what you tried to control can't be controlled. And for some, that can be a daily emotion. It's difficult navigating hard things. But how you consistently react to the unexpected determines your character.

If someone cuts you off in traffic, you can honk your horn or just let them pass. If you honk your horn, swear, and get angry *every* time, that is your character. That shows you are not able to balance your emotions when you feel you have been wronged.

Now, this doesn't mean you should be happy all the time or "peace and blessings" to every injustice, but you should be aware that things won't always go your way. People will hurt you and life will stress you out. However, you get to decide how you react. You get to choose what's *worth* your reaction. In the midst of the twists, turns, and unmet expectations, how do you want to live?

I learned the way to balance anger is to understand your triggers. Pinpoint what sparked the emotion. Was it yelling, lying, or being criticized? Your emotional response is based on the way you learned to cope with hardships. Knowing both can help you see where you might be overly concerned and excusing or correcting others. The more you know about yourself, the more you can talk about why you feel a certain way, what it's bringing up for you, and how you want to move forward.

When you feel you have been wronged, lean on these affirmations to remind you that it will be okay.

* * *

Do you prefer to be right or be happy?

MARIANNE WILLIAMSON

I have to be honest. I'm a know-it-all, or at least that's what my family and friends say when I'm being stubborn. The truth is, I get so fixated on "I know what I know" that it is hard for me to let another opinion in. Or that's how it feels to the person I'm talking to. Next thing you know, they have to accept my opinion as fact or just say, "Okay," and drop it. How exhausting.

But I didn't realize the impact of my actions until I was deep in a conversation with a new friend. It was like an out-of-body experience. All of a sudden, I could see what my friends were desperately trying to tell me.

One night, we were up late talking about our unpublished books. As a fellow writer, he expressed interest in the self-publishing process. I gave him some information, then asked whether he would like to be a part of my review process. He agreed, then immediately suggested a different process. (Now, don't make me mad.)

Prior to our conversation, I had taken a course by Dr. Paris Woods, the national bestseller of *Black Girl's Guide to Financial Freedom*. In her course, she explained in detail the process, cost, benefits, and downsides of self-publishing versus traditional publishing. I spent the following two weeks hyper-fixating on the process. When did I want to publish? How would I categorize my book? Who would I ask to be my beta readers, or people who read my unpolished copy? In true program management fashion, I laid out my plans for the next six months in Microsoft Excel. I was ready.

So, when someone I'd just met questioned me about a tried-and-true process that I'd spent weeks mapping out, I was irritated. Not emotionally upset, but internally, my mind was spinning. As he continued to give me his opinion, he asked me why I wanted to have my beta readers give me the most critical input, instead of a developmental editor.

Now, up until this point, I'd never heard of a developmental editor. In the process laid out to me, I was told I would need a copy editor and proofreader. So, now I was sitting on the rooftop looking skeptically at someone who obviously knew something I didn't. (I hate that feeling. As if you are on the outside of a joke or an exclusive club. It's very pick-me energy, but when it comes to data, I want to be picked! Is that cringe? Let's move on.)

I mean, it all checked out. He was a rising fiction author who had spent the past two years working on his manuscript and connecting with industry professionals at conferences across the country. He'd been through what I was going through, yet I was questioning whether *he* knew what *I* knew. (People are funny like that. When we are so deep in our ego, no one can tell us anything.)

The gag was, I didn't know that much. As he was speaking, I was typing in Google, "What is a developmental editor?" and "Developmental editor vs. copy editor." When Google AI confirmed what he'd said, I had the humbling thought, *I really don't know what I don't know.* Turns out the work I wanted my beta readers to do was the exact job description of a developmental editor. To my surprise, there were people whose job was to give me advice on the flow and readability of my content. I was flabbergasted. Honestly, I felt dumb, dismissive, and exactly what my friends and family said I was: stubborn.

When I looked up from my phone, I noticed the silence was deafening. A quote from Marianne Williamson's book *The Law of Divine Compensation* popped into my head:

"Do you prefer to be right or be happy?"

It's an internal question about whether the point you are defending is more important than the outcome you desire.

In my case, someone wanted to help me, and I just wanted to prove I knew what I knew, instead of being happy that someone believed in me enough to give me their honest feedback. I felt so silly. Why was I so defensive about a process I'd just learned? I mean, I was going to war for it. And it wasn't right or necessary. But I'm thankful I'm surrounded by people who can be a mirror to me in a safe environment. He never yelled or forced his opinion onto me. Instead, he reminded me that it was my book and I should choose the process that worked best for me.

At the end of the night, I shared my gratitude for him openly sharing his opinion. I'd had no idea that the help I needed existed outside of traditional publishing. I felt more empowered by taking his approach. This led to him being willing to share more about what he had learned from his author journey.

That day, I chose curiosity. I chose to be open to the possibility of being wrong. And because of that, I learned more about myself and the world around me. Just because I knew *a* way to do something didn't mean I knew *all* the ways to do it. It didn't mean that my way was the best way of doing it. Remaining curious sparked infinite possibilities. It allowed for growth, community, and connection to happen. For both of us.

As I sat with why I was so stubborn about certain topics, specifically with proving things that I believed to be true, I realized it was rooted in workplace trauma. For years, I was in spaces where I wasn't the expert and felt like a beginner. In an effort to prove I was knowledgeable, I had to prove *what* I knew and *how* I knew it. Over time, that habit went beyond the workplace. What started as a trauma response to prove my qualifications turned into a personality trait. And not a good one.

When I find myself getting ready to go back and forth with someone, it is important for me to pause and reflect. I withhold speaking and think about what I want the outcome of that conversation to be: being right or being happy for the exchange of knowledge. One leads with curiosity, while the other leads with defensiveness. One could be an insightful interaction, while the other could turn into a full-blown argument. And when I sit with those options, I trade in my anger for happiness.

And you should, too.

Realizing why you move the way you do empowers you to make better decisions in the moment. Once you know your triggers (such as getting asked questions you aren't ready for) and patterns (such as talking over people to prove your point), you're better equipped to change your outcomes. You are able to shape any moment of contention into one of understanding. And that will serve you at work, at home, and even at the family reunion.

Start by bringing awareness to the moment. Remind yourself who you are with and what you want. The next time you're preparing for a family gathering, say to yourself:

Hey, girl. Before you get too deep into this conversation, remember there is no need to defend your position here. You are amongst friends and family, so you can stand down. Resist the urge to prove your intelligence, legitimacy, and worth. The people who truly see you will not need to be convinced of your value. So, take a deep breath and choose happiness. If you're interested, ask questions. If you're not, just listen.

Anger is an emotion you will constantly experience if you always want to be right. You will find yourself being defensive in spaces where you were meant to breathe comfortably. When you choose curiosity, you sit comfortably knowing that every conversation and connection is an opportunity to learn more about others and yourself. It takes the pressure off you to prove something. Instead, you can just exist—right or wrong. You can hear the opinions of others and know it is not your place, or in your best interest, to change the minds of others. Be a vessel of information, not a martyr.

Affirmation: Do you prefer to be right or be happy?

Application: Draw back to this affirmation when you feel the need to get your point across. Use it to remain rooted in the fact that your opinion is just that, an opinion. It is not a law or a fact and does not need to be proven to anyone. With the release of that weight, you can finally sit back and relax. You can finally be an observer in your own life, identifying habits to start, continue, or drop while appreciating people for who they are.

Exploration:

1. When you are having a heated discussion with a family member, friend, or spouse, how do you feel: attacked or curious?
   a. If you feel attacked, what are they saying that's different from what you believe?
      ii. Can you plainly state that difference and be curious about why their opinion is different?
   c. If you feel curious, is the topic more important than your relationship?
      iv. There is no right or wrong answer, but it's important to know the answer to determine whether you prefer to be right or be happy.

* * *

Do you want to be bitter or be better?

MARIANNE WILLIAMSON

Have you ever got into an argument with your parents, and halfway through the conversation, they start making valid points, but you have spent hours building your case on why they are wrong and cannot bring yourself to admit that what they are saying makes sense for their actions. No? Yeah, me neither.

I mean, how embarrassing is it to know that the theatrics that we made up in our mind were demolished by a logic that wasn't our own? How embarrassing is it to spend hours in the shower thinking about all the ways they have wronged us, only for the day to come when they spend two seconds unraveling our thesis? (Oh, I'm cringing as well.)

At the peak of my depression, I became extremely angry with my maternal grandma. I wanted to be left alone—which I do not recommend in a season of depression. Yet, she wanted to talk and console me. She didn't know what was going on, but she knew something wasn't right. So, she reached out—consistently—after I had communicated I needed space. After a week of no response to her calls and messages, she became angry too.

Several months passed by with no contact. It was unusual for us because she was the woman who raised me. We were closer than close. But this time, I didn't have the energy to tend to anyone's emotions but my own.

Then, I decided to take a trip home to Southwest Florida. Usually, I'd stay with my paternal grandmother, or Grammy as I like to call her. This time wasn't any different. My first night in town was peaceful. Grammy wasn't the type to pry, so I got by without answering anything too personal regarding my mental health. However, that privacy didn't last long.

My grandmas have been best friends since I was a child. They usually saw each other four times a week. So, the next day we went to my maternal grandmother's house. I really didn't want to, but I knew I would have to face her one day. (I'm not telling you this as if she was my arch enemy or something.)

When we arrived at the house, Grammy walked through the door first. "What's going on in here?" she said jovially. Grandma replied. Then I greeted everyone in the house. "Good morning!" everyone replied—except her. As I got closer to the kitchen, she did her best to avoid eye contact with me. She walked past me, again, without acknowledgement. She had an attitude. And honestly, I didn't know why. But it felt so cold and harsh that I had to leave. I couldn't handle the emotional load, so I went to the beach to decompress.

When I got there, I plopped on my towel and let the heat and suffocating humidity consume me. Finally, a piece of peace. But it was short-lived. I couldn't stop thinking about my grandma's reactions. I thought, *How could she be mad that I didn't want to communicate on her terms?* It wasn't making sense to me. I decided to journal my emotions before dipping my foot in the warm salt water. As my feet sank into the ocean, I put my hands on my hips, tilted my head back, and let out a deep sigh. "Ahhhhhh . . ." I needed that.

When I got back to the house, I decided to address the elephant in the room.

"Why are you mad?" I asked when it was finally just the two of us.

"You told me not to talk to you ever again," she stated calmly.

"No," I snapped, "I said I didn't want to talk *right now* and I'd reach out when I was ready."

"Well, I just wanted to check on you."

"Well, I didn't want to talk. I was severely depressed, and I didn't want to tell you that!" I exclaimed with frustration in my voice.

"Well, that's all you needed to say. I would have understood."

I hated that she made it seem so simple. That expressing emotions in a Black family was the easiest thing in the world. It wasn't. Emotional vulnerability is usually met with ridicule, shame, and questions at family gatherings. It's exhausting. But here she was, wanting to provide the unexpected: clarity and comfort.

At that moment, it was hard to sit with her words. I was angry and hurt. I wanted my emotions and actions to be validated. No,

I wanted them to be justified. My emotions were too built up. I stormed out, leaving more anticipation in the room.

For days, I thought about that interaction. How was her reaction more justified than mine? How could she not see where I was coming from? As I journaled about my trip, as I do every vacation, I stumbled across an old entry. It was a quote from a book my therapist recommended when I was dealing with resentment. The quote was

"Do you want to be bitter or better?"

It was a question I'd read in *The Law of Divine Compensation* by Marianne Williamson. Marianne was talking about anger and how we can cling so tightly to narratives and old wounds that we block the flow of love.

It was thought-provoking when I first heard the question, but it was revealing when I had to answer it. When presented with a situation to be better, I chose bitterness. I chose to hold on to my anger and frustration for a little while longer. Why? Because I was overwhelmed by emotion. Choosing better would have required me to get to the root of my depression. It would have required me to acknowledge the pent-up anger and resentment I had. Not just for Grandma but for other relationships I was grieving as well. I wasn't ready for that. I wasn't ready to be better. And it cost me. I lost precious time with my grandma: sleep, memories, and the maternal comfort I desperately needed.

There was another way, a better way. Here's what I have learned since:

1. **Start the conversation.** If you deem the relationship important and want it to continue, put your ego aside and initiate the con-

versation. Healing takes place when we take action. If you are avoiding the conversation, you are delaying your peace of mind.

2. **Listen to their story.** When we are tied up in our own emotions, we rarely consider that there is a different and simultaneous story happening. Or that our story isn't the only truth. Take the time to understand their intention for you. We can quickly end up in a battle with ourselves, and the other person, when we refuse to see an intention outside of our own. Listen to how their intention drove their actions, then communicate yours.

3. **Communicate your feelings and actions.** Even when it is hard, take the time to communicate what is going on with you. Even if it's *"I don't want to talk about it right now, but I am sad and need some space."* Communicate your feelings along with your planned action. While you may know the feelings that drove you to that action, the other party doesn't. That leaves them to come to their own, oftentimes incorrect, conclusions about why you are acting a certain way. Clear up misconceptions early with communication.

4. **Choose better.** Choosing better doesn't mean being "the bigger person" for someone else's benefit. It means choosing peace, clarity, and healing for you. Every action you take costs you something—time, sleep, money, or sometimes the relationship. Are you willing and ready to pay the cost of your ego dwelling on perceived injustices? Is it *worth* your relationship?

You're the only one who can decide whether you want to remain bitter or be better. It's an active choice, meaning you have to do something in order to get it. Either cling to your old wounds or get better in your relationship, fitness journey, or career. I hope you choose better.

Affirmation: Do you prefer to be bitter or better?

Application: Draw back to this affirmation whenever your ego is taking over. Use it to remain rooted in the fact that you can control only what you do and how you react. Are you showing up honestly, with integrity and an open mind? If not, choose differently. Be the person who can admit their faults, even if the admission is to yourself. Be better.

Exploration:
1. What are you bitter about right now?
2. What do you keep thinking about over and over?
3. Do you have a list of all the wrongs against you?
    a. If so, you are holding resentment.
4. What do you need to get rid of the list?
    a. Is it an apology, a thank you, or maybe quality time?
5. Has this happened more than once?
6. Is this a pattern of yours or others?
7. How can you express to your friend, partner, or colleague what you need right now?

* * *

Let people be people.

BEST FRIEND

I used to think friendships lasted forever. That they were the one stable relationship we would have in our lives. If everything changed, your homegirls would be there with you till the end. Well, that wasn't true. Or should I say, it's not *always* true.

What I learned was that I had a tight grip on my friends. As we changed, I didn't let the relationship change with us. Instead, I tried to control everything: the narrative, their reactions, and our reality. I didn't know how to let my idea of relationships go. Because I didn't know how to let people move like the seasons do—in and out of alignment. But I had to learn.

The pandemic changed things, in people and relationships. For seven days a week, people had to sit with themselves for an extended period of time. That resulted in a lot of people realizing that who they thought they were was not who they actually were. And the persona they were portraying was no longer the image they wanted to maintain. Everyone was finally becoming their authentic selves.

This shifted one of my friendships in ways I didn't expect.

Alicia was one of my closest friends during the pandemic. We came together by chance but stayed together due to shared interests and proximity. In the latter part of the pandemic, she decided to move away. She often shared how her family didn't show up for her during life changes, so I offered to visit her once she got settled. We set a date and stayed in touch.

The week before the trip, she kept emphasizing everything she had to do because I was coming. I offered to postpone, but she declined. The day before my flight, I called to coordinate logistics, and she repeated how it was overwhelming having someone stay with her. I didn't know she felt like that. It was the first time she had ever mentioned it. I responded with, "I know you don't always say directly how you feel, but if it's too much, I can just cancel. It's not a problem." She scoffed and screamed, "You think just because you go to therapy you know everything!" Then she hung up. My jaw dropped as I looked at my phone move from an ongoing call to my screensaver. Shocked was an understatement. We had never argued before, nor had I said anything that warranted that response. I picked up my jaw—and spirit—unlocked the phone, and canceled the flight.

That moment haunted me for days. *Was I out of line? Was I asking too much?* I soon began questioning whether I was a good friend. Theoretically, yes. But was I being a good friend in *that* situation? Did I cross an invisible line that nobody had dared to tell me about? I was spiraling in anger, confusion, and pain.

I turned to my best friend, Coco, for advice. We went to a new Mexican restaurant and sat on their back patio. It was sunny, sixty degrees, and perfect for a "come to Jesus" moment. I gave her the play-by-play and asked for her *honest* opinion. "Am I wrong? What am I missing?" As I waited for her to tell me all the ways I was in the wrong, she simply asked clarifying questions. I loved that about her—always leading with curiosity. I further explained what had happened before and after the call. I ended my rant with, "Maybe she is going through something and she is just stressed. It has never happened before, and I'm sure it won't happen again."

Coco listened to me with her eyes squinted, head tilted, and eyebrows raised. It was the universal girl code for "whatever you are saying has some holes in it." She explained that even if she didn't agree with something I said, she would never yell or hang up on me—not someone she loved and cared for. She further explained that I was trying to take accountability for Alicia's actions. I was trying to make something that wasn't okay, okay. (I'd never had someone call me in like that.) I was avoiding being angry about it because I didn't think I had the right. Then, she confirmed what I desperately needed to hear: "Sister, you weren't wrong or asking for too much. You were simply asking the wrong person."

I cried amongst the trees, tacos, and my favorite person. I had been holding those emotions in, suffocating because I felt I couldn't talk to anyone about it. I thought I was avoiding the conversation because I didn't want to change anyone's opinion about Alicia due to my individual experience. Honestly, I was avoiding talking about it because *I* didn't want to think or feel differently about her. So, I excused her behavior and the assumptions that deeply hurt me.

Whenever I tried to understand people's motives or excuse their actions, Coco would humbly remind me:

Let people be people.

Meaning stop trying to control people. They are going to treat you the best way they know how. If that's not enough for you or what you want, let them go. Let them do them. Don't chase, beg, or try to change them. Accept them for who they are, who they want to be, and what they want to do. Let people be people.

When we allow others to authentically show up as themselves, we bring awareness to a few things: 1. What *they* want to do versus what *we* want them to do; 2. How they speak and respond to us—without coercion; and 3. Situations and relationships for what they really are. Something. Or nothing. But that clarity only comes when we give away the control. When we allow *them* to show *us* who they are and who they *want* to be.

If you have been wronged, be angry. Feel all the emotions. Cry about it. Sulk in it. It's completely normal and the right thing to do. When you are done crying, let people be people. Move out the way and let them be an active or inactive participant in your life.

Be aware of how others treat you without your telling them to. Notice how people apologize. Did they blame you for their actions? Did they even apologize? Did they take ownership? Did they offer to make it right? Did they ask you what you would have liked to occur instead?

You do yourself a disservice if you interact with people solely because of the history y'all built and not the quality of the current relationship. You strain the relationship when you try to make someone fit an older version of themselves, and they do the same to you.

Affirmation: Let people be people.

Application: Draw back to this affirmation when you are upset about how you are being treated by those closest to you. Use it to remain rooted in the fact that they are just people. They are guaranteed to hurt and disappoint you. They are guaranteed to not always get it right when it comes to handling you with care. Let them know. Tell them they hurt you. Tell them they have fallen short of your expectations. Then, allow them to do things differently. If they meet your needs, great! If they don't, let them go.

Exploration:
1. How has your friend, family, or coworker hurt you?
2. What did you expect from them, and how does that differ from what took place?
3. How can you tell them what you need? Practice articulating these feelings.
4. In the event they can't provide you with what you need, are you willing to stop asking?
5. Are you willing to accept that they are showing up as their best selves?

* * *

Forgiveness only needs one person. Reconciliation needs two.

DR. HENRY CLOUD

One thing about it and two things for sure: I'm going to stay in an unhealthy relationship—allegedly. Not necessarily for the plot, but for the apology. I need a verbal acknowledgement of wrongdoing and a promise of changed behavior. Most of my adult life, I would wait by the phone for something that often never came. I could put it on the child abandonment issues or being a parentified child, but as I got older, I realized I was looking for something no one could give me.

At this point in my life, I was navigating my grandpa's death and my relationship ending—again. So, I had a lot of overwhelming emotions. I was tired of pretending to be happier than I was. I hadn't been exposed to therapy or journaling yet, so I was hoping and praying I'd find some help soon. Then one day I was in the airport, and I saw *Changes That Heal* by Dr. Henry Cloud in my favorite shade of blue, promising "Four Steps to a Happier, Healthier You." I said, "Yup! That's for me," and speed walked to the checkout line.

Fast forward to night three of reading. I was on my third book break because Dr. Cloud was too much in my business. Exposing my pain, truths, and fears to me? In front of me? I felt violated. I felt ashamed. I felt seen.

When I got back in bed from my mental break, I immediately read

"Forgiveness only needs one person.
Reconciliation needs two."

I slammed the book shut. I flung aside the covers, stood up, and placed my hands on my hips. I was trying to collect my thoughts, but I couldn't. I was too stunned to speak. My jaw was on the floor! Again, this was before I had a therapist, so I didn't know how to deal with truth bombs. Balancing my emotions looked like me looking embarrassed in front of an imaginary *Abbott Elementary* camera until I regained my composure.

When Dr. Cloud said that, I was immediately transported back in time. My first and most memorable experience with forgiveness was in my second year at college. I had just had the best summer ever, and my high school best friend was moving to my college town. In the fall, we would be living together, and life would be just like we had planned it at fifteen years old. (I was so wrong.)

What ended up happening after we'd moved in together was drama for your mama. (I do not recommend living with your friends. For the sake of your relationship, just be neighbors.) I noticed she started doing things with our new friends she'd never done before. I couldn't understand it. It was people pleasing at its finest, or maybe it was discovery. We were two eighteen-year-olds in a new city, learning what freedom was. But the situation turned into a "she said" amongst our friends, which led to a big argument and her moving out. It was one of the hardest experiences I've been through and shaped the way I interacted in female relationships. I developed a deep insecurity around my perception and the need to prove my "innocence." I started overexplaining whenever I felt wronged or misunderstood. It was the birth of my own people-pleasing journey.

I went into a deep depression after that experience. I didn't talk to my friends for four to five months. Despite their calls to hang out, let it go, and in some cases "beat her ass," I avoided all interactions. It was hard. I leaned heavily on God during this period. I remember asking Him to help me through it. His response was to read the gospel of Matthew. I obliged.

My goal was to learn how to move and live like Jesus, a man who faced the ultimate persecution and humiliation. I wanted to know how He did it. What was His secret?

I learned three fundamental things from the Gospel:

1. Revenge is the Lord's. There is no need to get your lick back when God is in control. Trust that "they will be dealt with."
2. God's forgiveness is conditional. He will not forgive what you can't forgive.
3. If you are holding someone to a wrongdoing every time you see them, you have not forgiven them. Forgiveness is letting go so God can move in your favor.

And in that situation, He did just that. The week I let go of the situation, released control over the results, and stopped holding anger in my heart was the same week I unexpectedly received an apology call. He truly is a miracle worker.

So, as I replayed "Forgiveness only needs one person; reconciliation needs two," I thought about that fall semester in college. I was desperately looking for reconciliation. I was looking for her to acknowledge how crazy and wrong the situation was so we could move forward. After all, she was my best friend.

However, this required two separate people to heal on the same timeline *and* come to a joint conclusion about the next steps. If I know anything about healing, rarely is it done in tandem with someone. Usually, healing happens for one person and then later, sometimes months or years later, for the other person. It is not a group exercise.

Forgiveness only requires you to acknowledge what happened and say, "It's okay. I forgive you." It does not require an audience. Just a simple, but oftentimes very difficult, belief that everything is going to be okay. That the unwanted situation happened to you, but instead of choosing to be bound by it, you chose to forgive.

The anger, confusion, and frustration you're feeling are not for you to reconcile; it's God's work. The plans you made to "show them" are not for you to execute; it's God's work. So move out the way and let the Man work!

He forgave you. With all that you have done and all that your friends and family said was "unforgivable," He forgave you. So, forgive them. A thousand times over, forgive them. It only requires you.

Affirmation: Forgiveness only needs one person. Reconciliation needs two.

Application: Draw back to this affirmation when you feel the need to reconcile wrongdoing. Use it to remain rooted in the fact that you don't need two people to get the results you are looking for. You can experience peace when you let go of the need for an acknowledgement, an apology, an answer, or a way forward.

Exploration:
1. What situation left you with an immense need for an apology?
2. What will the apology change for you?
3. How will it allow you to move forward? What do you want to change?
4. Is forgiveness possible without an apology?
   a. What would it look like to go on living, thriving, and being without reconciliation?
5. What can you release in order to gain what you really want?

* * *

Every relationship is an assignment.

THERAPIST

When things didn't go the way I'd planned, I tried to rationalize what had happened and where it had gone wrong. I combed through every injustice and applied meaning to it—one way or another. Over time, I realized that not only was that pointless, but it also didn't serve me the way I thought it would.

I thought that if I understood where things had gone wrong, I could save the relationship or, at the very least, know what *not* to do in my other relationships. Turns out, overanalyzing your trauma is not the solution for being trauma-free. (Who would have thought? Not me!) It was just a distraction from the wounds that were forming. It was a defense mechanism against having to acknowledge and actually feel the pain I was experiencing. It didn't get to the root of what I really needed: security in knowing the relationship mattered and, more importantly, that I mattered to the other person.

I remember the first time that I felt this need but couldn't put it into words. I was just coming off a bachelorette trip to Colombia, where a few things had happened that I didn't like, specifically around safety and communication. I knew that I would have a conversation with my best friend and everything would be good. I mean, we weren't new to difficult conversations. We'd been friends for over a decade, and based on past experiences, we would talk about how we were feeling, apologize, start crying about how much we respected each other's opinions, and grow deeper in our relationship.

Well, that's not how the cookie crumbled. What transpired was three months of pure agony—on both sides. As we started unpacking what had happened and how we felt, it became long episodes of emotional dumping. We were so caught off guard by how the other felt that the following conversations became "I can't believe you said that. It hurt my feelings. I think that . . ."

We began talking *at* each other and not *with* each other. Responding to every point made instead of acknowledging the pain and purpose *behind* the point.

We had multiple calls about how we could move forward. Each ended with, "Can this be fixed before my wedding?" (A question that made me feel as though fixing our image was more important than repairing our actual relationship.) The reality was that it couldn't be. The more I talked, the more I realized my pain spanned fifteen months. There were situations I'd never brought up because I thought they were one-offs, so I labelled the pain as temporary.

I mean, this was someone I considered an actual sister. How could I hold anger or resentment against her? Over the years, she had shown up for me when no one else did, across cities, states, and seasons. She was intentional, kind, thoughtful, incredibly smart, determined, and absolutely feisty. She was my girl. A true ride-or-die if I ever needed a physical example of one. But that wasn't enough to carry the relationship.

After our third call, I realized that how she was showing up no longer felt supportive for me. We were both navigating a lot, in different ways.

For me, a lot had happened the week of the bachelorette trip. Within seven days, I coordinated bachelorette logistics, moved apartments, had my car stolen and recovered, and traveled twelve hours to the bachelorette destination. I was overwhelmed and exhausted.

Then I became hypervigilant on safety: mentally, physically, and emotionally. I was still processing my new normal, trying to grasp a reality where unthinkable things happened at unthinkable times to everyday people—including me. It was a lot, but I acknowledged the possible impact it had had on my emotions and perception.

For her, she was about to get married to the love of her life. Not only was she planning a wedding and navigating a demanding career, but she was also dealing with everyday life. A lot of new and good things were happening for her. And I loved that. She deserved every beautiful thing God could provide a human in this lifetime. What I didn't love was the lack of acknowledgement that all these changes had an impact on how she was showing up in her other relationships. When I shared my concerns, they were met with "That never happened," or "I wouldn't do that."

It was tough, but I believed I was tougher. So, we continued to push through.

What transpired for me was months of not sleeping or eating because I was so consumed with things that had been said in our conversations. She'd gone so far as to say I was making up the fact that she was going to let me walk back to the Airbnb by myself in the middle of the night in Colombia, or my wanting to even leave the club was selfish (based on her psychology class at college). Girl, I was doubling down on therapy sessions and crying in the shower every day. It wasn't good.

I only realized how much of a toll it was taking on me when I went to a chiropractor session and decided to walk home. The entire walk home, I was consumed with a conversation we'd had the previous weekend. I looked down at my Apple watch and saw that I had walked for forty-five minutes. Forty-five minutes! I was so engulfed by the situation that I didn't even realize how much time had passed. I was no longer in reality, or the present. I was consumed with the past. I was deep in creating should-have scenarios for a situation that could not be changed.

As much as we wanted to get better, I just didn't see a way to do it. All the methods we had used in the past to grow our relationship became the primary examples of how our relationship was different. How *we* had become different. It was a deeply painful experience for both of us.

Once the text messages progressed to passive aggression, blame, and entitlement, I said, "No more." Enough was enough. She felt disrespected. I felt disrespected, and the only thing that could heal us was time that we didn't have.

Tears streamed down my face as I typed up my final message, expressing my gratitude and love for our relationship and her as a person. I didn't want the relationship to end, but I knew I couldn't go another day living as I was. I knew that I no longer felt safe in the relationship, and that was what I craved the most in that season of my life.

Coincidentally, I had a therapy session that day with Amina. It was a video call, but that didn't stop me from bawling my eyes out as if I was on her couch. I let her know what I had decided and how I felt: crushed, but at the same time, as if I could finally breathe again because a decision had been made. She met my teary gaze with a comforting smile and said,

> "Every relationship is an assignment and an opportunity to learn more about ourselves."

Meaning all relationships are meant to teach you something. They have purpose even when you can't see it.

My therapist acknowledged the parts of me that felt like a horrible friend for not being able to make it work weeks before the wedding, while acknowledging the reality that I had shown up, even at the expense of my mental health, for months, trying to repair our relationship. She reminded me that although it hadn't gone as planned, there was still value in trying. There was still purpose and intention in the relationship that was activated when I showed up. When we showed up for each other to have tough, painful, and many times, agonizing conversations.

In true fashion, she ended our session with a thought-provoking question: "Are you open to new relationships? Even after the last few months that you've had, would you be open?" I was emotionally exhausted, and the thought of navigating another relationship made me tense, but I lied and said, "Yeah! I am open." Then she gave me some more words of encouragement and journal prompts to comfort me until our next session.

In learning to treat relationships as assignments, I had to remove my expectations around the final outcome of the relationship. In order to do that, I had to remove the blame and shame for their wrongdoings along the way. I had to stop tracking their wrongdoings to use against them as a basis for my discontent with the relationship. If something happened that I didn't like, I could talk to them about it, but I couldn't hold it against them.

Similarly, I could not change how they treated me. In fact, I wanted to free myself of the responsibility of trying to change others to meet my needs and desires. I wanted to understand and appreciate who they were without interfering or nagging at them for something I didn't like or "would never do." I had to let people be people.

Finally, I had to remove the desire to overanalyze things that had already happened and couldn't be changed. I had to stop "fighting for what God did while at war with what God is doing," as Sarah Jakes Roberts would say.

I had to acknowledge that assignments are temporary and specific to a time. Only when the environment and conditions are right is fruit produced, new life born, and purpose revealed. It is not all year round but specific to a time and place. It's the same with relationships. At the right time, and during a specific season, you will get everything you need from them. They will give you joy, purpose, love, stress, grief, and most importantly, humanity. Relationships will be everything you didn't know you needed—good and bad, when you need it the most.

You learn how to appreciate the assignment when you are able to ask yourself, "What did I learn? What was my assignment?" Because it was never about them anyway.

Affirmation: Every relationship is an assignment.

Application: Draw back to this affirmation when you are beating yourself up over a relationship that hurt you. Use it to remain rooted in the fact that no experience is wasted or without purpose. Each one teaches us something about others and ourselves. Usually, knowing the latter leads to changed behavior and different outcomes.

Exploration:
1. When was your last difficult relationship?
2. What made that relationship so challenging?
3. What did that challenge teach you about what you need in that type of relationship?
4. Was this something that you have been struggling with in the past?
5. How can you communicate that need early to allow it to be met?

* * *

Thoughts are not instructions.

THERAPIST

Let my friends tell it: I used to consider every form of communication as a sign to connect with people from the past.

- A dream (Because maybe God was trying to tell me something, like apply grace.)

- An out-of-the-blue call (Because maybe they are sorry and want to fix things.)

- A sermon (Because maybe God thinks I didn't get it and need divine intervention.)

- Or an unexpected email (Because maybe they have finally seen my point and want to apologize.)

It really didn't matter. I was going to make amends, apply grace, and forgive and forget. Even if they wronged me in unforgivable ways. That was my life, until it wasn't.

When I read *The Mountain Is You* by Brianna Weist, my patterns began to change. Specifically, when I learned the importance of operating on intuitive versus intrusive thoughts. Intuitive thoughts are fleeting thoughts or rationale that give you clarity and peace while benefiting those around you. They are like ah-ha moments that come to you in the shower, on your commute to work, or during an engaging conversation. Intrusive thoughts are "loud" and repetitive. They cause you anxiety and fear and impact your emotional well-being. They're usually the things you can't get out of your head. You start replaying every detail of an interaction. Then you draw a conclusion based on the one-sided conversation you just had. (Is this delusion entering the chat? Whoops!) The intrusive part about it is that even after you draw a conclusion, you continue to replay the scenario as if *nothing* was decided. It becomes obsessive.

I couldn't wait to tell my therapist about my latest read. Really, I couldn't wait to fact-check the research with her. "Is this a real thing? Is it true?" I needed more information before I changed my whole life. (I'm only being slightly dramatic.)

When I finished updating her on my life and latest read, she smiled into the camera and said,

"Yeah, because thoughts aren't instructions. Right?"

I tilted my head to the right in confusion, stumbling to gather my thoughts.

Right? Since when? Who said that? And why didn't anyone tell me? Up until that point, all my actions stemmed from a thought I had. So how was I supposed to know which thoughts to act upon and which to leave as thoughts? (I felt like that meme of the confused woman with a complicated math problem above her head. Just watching the math not math.)

We had to pause my incoming thoughts because I yapped until the end of our session. I left that session with more questions than answers.

At the time, I was getting to know someone who would love-bomb me, go missing, apologize, then do it again. I had a lot of intrusive thoughts and unpleasant words to share. I would let the "This reminded me of you" message sit unread in my text messages for days. Not because I was being cool, calm, and collected with my response. No. I was crashing out! The intrusive thoughts were screaming.

Why did he send me that, like I didn't ask him a direct question two days ago? And this ain't the first time. Does he think I'm one to be played with? Oh noo, baby. Not me. So, what are you going to say and do to remind him that you are not? Block him!

Yeah, it sounded crazy, but it felt crazier. I would obsess over every detail and every intention behind his messages. After an intense back-and-forth battle with myself, I would think, *Nah. That might be too far. If I block him, that would be giving away my power. I would be giving him the satisfaction of knowing that my feelings are hurt and I'm spiraling over some dusty guy.*

To avoid my ego being bruised externally, I excused his behavior. I reminded myself that life happens for everyone, and he was probably just busy. (The lies we tell ourselves are sickening.) I texted him a thumbs-up as if everything was okay. It wasn't, but people pleasing was my middle name, so I wasn't going to tell him that.

After going back to my therapist, she asked, "How much do you matter in collecting these experiences?" (Yikes! Amina didn't have to do me like that.) "You seem to have a high pain tolerance." (Girl, please step off my neck. It's suffocating.) I didn't have the words. The answer was obvious. I didn't matter in collecting those experiences. I was letting people treat me any kind of way. And that was a hard truth to sit with.

Here's what I learned: You can't hear the intuitive thoughts when you are in the thick of it. You must get out of your head and into your body. Here's how:

1. **Write out the facts.** Get a journal and write down in chrono-logical order what happened and how it made you feel. Write the action statement. Then, the emotion. "He disregarded my question. I feel overlooked and disconnected." Or "She took a long time to respond. I feel neglected." Try to avoid action + result + emotion + result. This is crashing out on paper. While it can be helpful to feel emotions, it's not for this exercise.

2. **Put some distance between you and the situation.** When you stop trying to force a response or answer, the intuitive thoughts get a chance to surface. During your quiet moments, subtle emotions will come to you. "X happened, and I didn't like it." "Y was said, and it made me feel Z." These are thoughts that stand on their own. They are not statements about what you would have, should have, or could have done—commonly known as crash outs. They are your true feelings. Your intuitive thoughts. Give them space to reveal themselves. Then, notice them and write them down.

3. **Assess.** When you see the actions and reactions very plainly and clearly on paper, you can objectively see what your next step could be. Ask yourself, "Is that what I want?" If the answer is yes, then go for it. If the answer is no, stand on business. You don't have to scream it from the rooftops, but the next time they message you, clearly and briefly state you are not interested in being friends, hanging out, or whatever it is you decide not to do.

Nobody wants drama in their life. But we must admit when *we* are the drama. (Oops!) Sometimes it's not about rewiring our thoughts but seeing them plainly. I can only do that when I write them down. I have a journal for the crash outs to feel my emotions, and I have a journal for the facts. When I step away from the facts (about what happened and how I felt about it—not the person) and see it for what it truly is, what does the data say? Now, what do I say? What do I want to do about it?

It's okay to want to message someone from the past when they have wronged you. Forgiveness takes on many forms, but don't forgive and forget. Don't forget how you feel and why. Break the cycle. Come out of your fantasy of what *could* be and back to the reality of what is.

People are what they repeatedly do. So, if you see something concerning on multiple occasions, trust the data. Trust yourself. A gut instinct doesn't need evidence. It doesn't even require a second thought. It only requires you to see and act.

Affirmation: Thoughts are not instructions.

Application: Draw back to this affirmation whenever your thoughts are louder than your voice. Use it to remain rooted in the fact that just because you thought about it doesn't mean you have to act upon it. Some thoughts are protective parts trying to rationalize or justify your pain. Use them as information, not fuel to crash out.

Exploration:
1. What am I constantly thinking about right now?
2. When I think about this, do I feel curious or angry?
3. When I feel this way, am I drawn to take action?
4. What's drawing me to act—compulsion or curiosity? (If you feel curious, it is probably an intuitive thought. If you feel anger or compulsion, it is likely an intrusive thought, and any action should be taken with caution.)

How Do I Overcome Anger?

Anger is a natural emotion. It's a reminder that something did not go the way you wanted or something unexpected happened. That's okay. That's information. You have the power to choose how you react when this emotion comes up. Will you let it derail your day, relationship, or life? Or will you hold it with care and give it your undivided attention? Anger fuels defensiveness and ego. If you let it go unchecked, you can end up saying and doing things you later regret.

The key to overcoming anger is acknowledging you are in a state of anger and communicating what you would have preferred to happen. If someone doesn't include you in the decision-making process, you can acknowledge that you are angry. Sit with the emotion. Then ask, "In the future, can we make those decisions together?" Feel, heal, then respond.

Choose curiosity over defensiveness. Shift the focus from proving your point to fostering peace and connection. Doing so shifts the narrative from someone personally attacking you to their responding with the best communication skills they have. That is how you can reduce your emotional reactivity.

And once you have a method to change your reaction, go back and understand what your anger was rooted in: past trauma, ego, or the desire to feel validated? Be honest. Ask yourself whether your need to be "right" was worth the potential harm to your relationships. Did your pride matter more than your peace? Be honest. Then, choose another way to express yourself. Choose another way to heal your inner wounds.

You balance anger when you remain observant, reflective, and open.

(Now, hold my hand.)

You are more than this emotion.

six

OVERCOMING RESENTMENT

when you can't shake the way you feel

Anger that isn't fully expressed or processed silently grows into resentment. It shows up when your parent, partner, coworker, or friend doesn't meet an expectation that you have. (Likely because you never told them.) Then, over time, you start to feel bitter, insulted, and angry.

You don't mean to, but it sort of just happens. They might ask you what's wrong, but sometimes you can't put your finger on it. You just know that you are secretly keeping score of what you've given, tolerated, or sacrificed in the relationship. And now, you are silently punishing them for it.

I get it. I don't always realize I'm holding resentment toward those I care about until we take a deep dive into what's going on. Only after a series of questions do I realize I expected something to happen that didn't. I expected them to know better or do better, and they didn't.

I learned that when I feel someone should just "get it" and they don't, I have unspoken expectations that I should either express or adjust through boundaries.

When you feel something isn't adding up, lean on these affirmations to remind yourself to go about the situation in a different way.

* * *

You can be grateful without feeling indebted.

JA'MARA WASHINGTON

Have you ever wanted something so bad that you prayed night and day for it? I mean, you went as far as asking your friends and family to pray on your behalf because you were determined for God to get the message. Then, when you finally received your blessing, you found out you didn't actually want the thing you'd prayed for. It's not what you thought it was going to be. So, you felt obligated to commit long-term because you didn't want to seem ungrateful. Like when you accepted a job after being laid off, then realized it was sucking the soul out of you, but you stayed because your family kept reminding you, "It's a job." Or when you meet your soulmate—perfect in every way, but you weren't emotionally ready for a relationship that required you to change. How about when you prayed to be a mother, but then you felt unequipped to be *anyone's* mom? So you felt ridiculous complaining about it being the hardest job known to man because you'd said it was your dream.

Yeah. Those "this is what I wanted, but I didn't know it was going to be like this" realizations hit me hard, too. Over time, I found myself faking the funk. Acting like I was happy for the blessing—because it was still a blessing, just maybe not for me. Then, my feelings of obligation turned into people pleasing: saying yes to every request, helping out whenever asked, and apologizing after every statement. I started abandoning my needs for others'. Every new opportunity was centered on proving I was grateful and appreciative for what others had done for me. It wasn't my intention, but it became my reality. And I only realized it after it was too late.

It was Spring 2021 when my homegirl Shayla told me about a new book she was reading on boundaries. Mind you, this is the same homegirl who recommended *Boundaries: When to Say Yes, How to Say No to Take Control of Your Life* by Dr. Henry Cloud and Dr. John Townsend. I thought that was the holy grail of holy grails, so my first response was, "Now wait a minute, Savannah. Slow down." I reminded her that Dr. Cloud and Dr. Townsend described the different types of boundaries through patient scenarios, how to apply them, and how they echoed the Word. I didn't see how anyone could top that. Shayla insisted that *Set Boundaries, Find Peace: A Guide to Reclaiming Yourself* by Nedra Glover Tawwab was different. She wrote as if she was talking to her homegirl and giving application methods that were different from the book I already loved. I was still skeptical. Two weeks later, my best friend Coco was raving about the same book and gifted me a copy. When I tell you Ms. Nedra Glover Tawwab had me questioning my entire life, I mean that.

During the pandemic, I switched careers and began working as a Technical Program Manager on an engineering team. I was hired because the team was growing fast and there were a lot of things that needed to be done to make sure they could grow efficiently. My manager trusted my expertise, so he let me work on whatever issues I thought needed solving. The autonomy allowed me to learn the pain points of the team, then use what I learned to create my own role. I loved it.

As I excelled in the role, more work was added to my plate. A few months in, my manager asked me to join a highly visible project. This meant high engagement and collaboration with the team—basically my superpower—so I said, "Count me in." My manager also needed someone to take over budgeting, development, operations, and customer engagement. I thought, *I'm still new and have time on my hands. Why not?*

Those yeses led to twelve- to fifteen-hour days. I was tired. Hell, some days I was exhausted, but I didn't mind because I was finally working on exciting work. On top of that, I had a dope manager, worked remotely, and could voice my opinion at work—which was *rare* for a Black woman. I felt as though I was finally living the American dream. Yet I found myself needing vacations and therapy to silence the work ideas and deadlines that constantly played in my mind.

What I didn't realize until I was reading the section about work in *Set Boundaries, Find Peace* was that I didn't have a work boundary. (Let's unclench our pearls together.) As Nedra explained the nature of burnout, I thought, *This is what I'm going through!* However, unlike her client, I didn't dislike my boss or have difficulty communicating how I felt to him. Or so I thought.

When you receive everything you could ever ask for, you can feel guilty for expressing when it's too much. It feels like ungratefulness or dissatisfaction.

When I transitioned to the tech industry, I was working remotely and with purpose. They were also paying me well. So I questioned how I could complain about any "little" thing that my team asked of me. I had learned from startups that long hours and an increased workload were part of walking in your purpose. And I had the ability and capacity to do it. Until I didn't.

You can't be everything to everyone all at once. If you are, you leave little space for you to show up for yourself.

As Nedra reminded me, there needed to be a balance between doing what I could and communicating when I couldn't. I was so concerned with being useful and polite that my needs became invisible. I got so used to wearing multiple hats in a startup environment that I didn't realize that it wasn't sustainable in a large company—until my body started screaming for a break.

The next morning, I turned on my favorite R&B playlist and stepped into the steaming hot shower. As the water hit my back, I kept thinking about how I was the "boundaries guru," yet hadn't realized I didn't have a work boundary. I thought I was *so* open and honest with my manager. But really, I wasn't being honest with myself. Then, as a subtle reminder and ah-ha, God said,

"You can be grateful without feeling indebted."

(Record scratch.)

I repeated it back to Him to make sure I'd heard Him correctly. "You can be grateful and not indebted?" Meaning I could be grateful for this amazing opportunity without feeling as if I had to accept every request my manager made. I was still a great employee, even if I didn't do everything, for everyone, all at once.

Feeling indebted was only building resentment for my blessing. It shifted my gratitude to overextension and bitterness. In order to let go of my resentment, I had to start communicating my needs, and not just my desires, to my manager. My desires led me to people pleasing—consistently saying yes, instead of honoring my time with an honest no.

To shift toward gratitude, I created a Work Breakdown Structure. Typically, it is used to show all the work and resources in a project. However, I used it to showcase where all my energy was going. Then, I used that diagram to prioritize my time with my manager.

Here's how you do it:

1. **Write down in Excel all the things you are working on.** The things in your job description and the side projects you may be doing for your team. Don't miss any details from your day-to-day. Your responsibilities will be in the first column. Then add who may have asked for the work and what value it holds. This will be in your second and third columns.

2. **Identify the value, requester, and owner of each responsibility.** This may look like "I review documents in our main database." The value could be "Make sure data is available and correct for the team." The requester may be your teammate, and the owner is currently you.

3. **Review the Work Breakdown Structure with your manager.** Schedule a one-on-one meeting to discuss your responsibilities. Go line by line to see whether your manager is aware of and agrees on the importance of those items. Share what work energizes you and what depletes you. Together, agree on what work you should stop, start, or continue doing. This will be in the last column of your spreadsheet. It's like your next steps.

Work Breakdown Structure					
Responsibility	Value	Impact Level	Requestor	Owner	Decision Required
Metrics Dashboard	Improve Insights	Medium	Manager	Myself	Stop
Brand Refresh	Enhance Perception	High	Teammate	Myself	Continue
International Launch	Expand Market	Medium	Director	Myself	Start
Community Playbook	Grow Advocates	Low	Teammate	Myself	Stop
Partner Integrations	Expand Reach	High	Manager	Myself	Continue

Figure 2: Work Breakdown Structure

My manager, being the amazing human that he was, was grateful for my communication and desire to share my work. To my surprise, many of the tasks that I took the initiative on, he didn't even know about. While it was great that I was solving problems for the team, they had minimal visibility and value at the executive level. In other words, they weren't the best use of my time. Knowing that my manager cared about my well-being beyond my work was refreshing. But defining the important things so I could reclaim my time was game-changing.

That day, I learned the value of being grateful and not feeling indebted. One felt empowering, and the other felt criminal. One was rooted in freedom, and the other in obligation. I was finally able to move in alignment, at work and beyond.

How often do we burn ourselves out trying to go above and beyond? Thinking we are changing the world, but really, no one knows what we are doing, and we are running ourselves dry.

Slow down. Appreciate the moment for what it is. You have more chances to show what you are capable of, but they'll never see it if you are doing too much and not taking care of yourself. Take the lunch break, midday nap, walk in the sun, or extended vacation. Go pick up your kids from school. After all, it's just work. You don't owe them every minute of your day. The work will be there when you get back—after you have prioritized your needs.

Affirmation: You can be grateful and not indebted.

Application: Draw back to this affirmation when you need a reminder that just because someone did something nice for you doesn't mean you owe them. Notice when you are saying yes to please others. Use it to remain rooted in the fact that you don't have to be everything to everyone. You have a limit, and it's worth communicating when that limit has been reached. It doesn't mean that it's forever, but right now you can't. And that's okay.

Exploration:
1. When was the last time you gave a reluctant yes?
2. What did they ask you?
3. What else did you have going on at the time that prevented it from being an eager yes?
4. What conditions do you need to provide an eager yes?
5. Do you feel comfortable communicating these thoughts and emotions with the person who asked something of you?
   a. If not, write down your responses so you are aware of when you are likely to give a reluctant yes.

* * *

Everyone starts in the lobby.

THERAPIST

I'm notorious for having a bunch of best friends. (Seriously, my manager jokes with me about it all the time.) Many of my relationships started in childhood or college. As time passed, I would meet someone who perfectly aligned with the stage of life I was in and added them to my list of best friends. For the longest time, I had nine best friends. Each one provided something different, which allowed me to have experiences that shaped my personality, preferences, and outlook on life. It was beautiful.

As I got older, I realized the aspect of relationships that I loved the most was emotional and physical availability. I loved being able to sit for hours with my friends, talking about all the things we'd learned, the ways life had changed, and how we still had time to change the world. I loved holding space for them to share their traumas, dreams, and lives. I especially enjoyed watching them grow over time, blossoming into well-rounded adults, parents, spouses, and disciples.

Quality time quickly became my favorite pastime. Sharing our lives over margaritas, bottomless brunch, oceanfront views, morning hikes, or international flights. It was the best part of being in our late twenties. However, these times became few and far between with my long-distance friendships. Our hangout sessions had to be planned and more intentional. For years, we made it work. But after five, or even ten, years, I noticed I was seeing some of my best friends only once a year. More importantly, I was seeing them only if I initiated the request to meet or came to a location that was convenient for them.

That reality was painful to think about. I had best friends who were reciprocating the effort to maintain the relationship, and then I had friends who would only reach out on my birthday. Yet they both held the best friend title. How could that be? How could I call someone my best friend if the friendship was not maintained? If I only talked to them once a year? If they only knew about my life because of social media highlights, how was our relationship any different from a friend or an associate?

I wrestled with those questions a lot. I often had people asking me why so-and-so was my best friend. And when I was honest, the only examples I could give were from years ago. I didn't have any current representations of how they had shown up for me in the past three, four, or five years. They liked my social media posts and tagged me in their Instagram story for my birthday, but they didn't show up physically or in ways that mattered. They were supportive of me, but they were no longer a part of my support system. I couldn't call them when something difficult was happening; I only felt comfortable giving them a recap of how I had navigated it on my own or with other friends.

And that hurt. When I thought about friends forever, I truly thought the way it started was the way it would always be. I can blame it on the way friendships are depicted in movies or the promises we made to each other in school, but I wasn't prepared for this reality check.

Resentment toward my best friends grew. I wrote down how I was feeling in my journal (no shocker there), but it wasn't helping, so I sat down with my therapist. She showed me a diagram where I was in the center of a circle and there were circles around me, explaining my relation to others. She then gave me homework to think about where my current relationships were in proximity to me. She explained,

"Everyone starts in the lobby."

This means that everyone couldn't receive immediate access to me or the benefits of me. There is a period where they are outside of my circle, or in the lobby, and I get to assess the level of access they get into the building. Not as a one-time experience, but a continual one. She told me to think about my relationships and draw my own diagram of where everyone stood in relation to me. I don't play around with introspective assignments, so I quickly got to work.

I created what I like to call a Community Map. It was a comparison diagram that showed who I was interacting with, what standard or expectation I was holding them to, and if that expectation was realistic. (Spoiler alert: this exercise changed my life!)

I started by writing out the different types of relational categories: best friends, close friends, friends, and associates. Then I categorized the people I had interacted with over the past six to twelve months. I listed their names under the categories, then put what my expectation was for each group. What activities do people in this category do? How do they act toward me? How do I act toward them? What type of information do I trust them with? Would I call them in the middle of the night? Would I travel with them? Would I get mad with them if we didn't speak in a month? What about six months? How do I expect them to show up for me? Do they naturally do that?

For example, my best friends are people I don't mind telling something I'm ashamed of. They are people I am *actively* doing life with. That includes travelling together, celebrating life milestones, and dilly-dallying to the max. They are people who intentionally show up for me without having to ask three or four times. I feel my safest around them.

Then I made a row of my expectations for each category. What things did I need or want from each group? Did I really care if my friends didn't reach out as much as my best friends? Did I care if my associates weren't intentional? This helped me get clear on what my resentment was rooted in. It helped me see which unmet expectations I had for each friend.

Lastly, I had to review the truth. While some best friends had met my needs in the past, they did not meet them currently. At this point in our journey, they aligned more with a close friend or an associate. Similarly, some friends that I thought were just friends were actually showing up in a close friend capacity.

The final step was placing everyone according to how they showed up. Not how I wanted them to, but how they embodied the values I placed on specific relationships.

I learned that expecting my best friends to always be my best friends was an unrealistic expectation. Silently, it was straining my relationships and me. In order to balance resentment, I had to get comfortable with mentally demoting and promoting my friends. I had to look at where the relationship was today and decide whether it still made sense to hold certain expectations of that person.

Community Map				
	Best Friends	Close Friends	Friends	Associates
Who fits this title?	Jessica, Josiah, Brittany	Sonia, Fernando, Stephanie, Mia	Kim, Isaiah	People from: College, Work, or Associations
How do they show up for you?	Call anytime. Trust with secrets. Travel together. Accounability partner.	Text anytime. Trust with most information. Travel together. Initiate conversations.	Support my business. Attend events together.	Connect me to opportunities, events or other people.
What do you need for each person to receive this title?	Intention Reciprocity	Communication Support	Trust Safety	Respect Safety
Does everyone show up this way?	No	No	Yes	Yes
If not, how should this category look based on your needs?	Mia, Jessica	Josiah, Brittany, Sonia, Stephanie	Fernando, Kim, Isaiah	People from: College, Work or Associations

Figure 3: Community Map

By objectively seeing where people stood, I was able to release the negative emotions I had for them. If I was mad someone never called me back, I could go to my Community Map and see that at that stage of our friendship, we'd become associates. I could verify that I didn't have an expectation for my associates to call me back. The relationship was touch-and-go, so the emotion I was feeling was unwarranted. The process of checking my emotions, regulating them, and resetting my expectations of others helped me release the built-up resentment I had toward my friends.

This process also helped with new relationships. Traditionally, I was quick to label someone as a friend. Then I would grow resentful when they didn't show up the way I felt a friend should. (Delusional? Absolutely!) I was still getting to know them, yet I was already holding them to a standard they didn't ask for. This caused unnecessary conversations, all because I was quick to hold people in positions they didn't ask to be in. I was quick to assign meaning before I defined connection.

"Everyone starts in the lobby" is about understanding where to direct your energy and emotions in relationships. It's about taking inventory of your expectations and checking yourself when you freely give people access that they don't need. When you can't shake how you feel about your friends, draw your own Community Map so you can determine why.

People can only meet your expectations when you figure out what you're expecting. This isn't an exercise to chastise your friends; it's an opportunity to be real with yourself. Relationships have unspoken expectations, and they are different for each person. Take the time to understand your wants, needs, and emotions more deeply. Take the time to assess what is the best use of your time and energy. It starts with understanding your relationships.

Affirmation: Everyone starts in the lobby.

Application: Draw back to this phrase when you need a reminder that relationships take time and take on many forms. Use it to remain rooted in the fact that relationships don't need to be defined within the first thirty seconds of knowing someone. You have to see their character first—not just hear about it. By witnessing the relationship and letting it ebb and flow through different experiences, both parties can become clear on who they are to each other, what the expectations could be, and where the relationship goes next. Even *if* that relationship changes over time.

Exploration:
1. When was the last time you met someone and immediately determined where they would fit in your life?
2. What did you expect from someone in that category?
3. Did they meet that expectation?
   a. If yes, for how long?
   b. If not, what did you learn about them over time that you didn't know initially?
      iii. Were there similar or different values? Interests? Communication styles?
4. Was the placement the same after one month, three months, or a year?
5. What did you learn about them?
6. How can you allow yourself more time to get to know them?
7. What strategies or boundaries do you want to adopt to make this happen?

* * *

There are no special relationships.

THERAPIST

As I continued to introduce boundaries into my life, my relationships began to change. Or should I say, I began to change in my relationships. As I became more honest about who I was and who I wanted to be, I noticed situations where I had double standards or loose boundaries. Meaning I would confidently address issues in one relationship, but I wouldn't in another. Why? I was scared to be perceived as controlling, bossy, demanding, and all the negative terms associated with expressing emotions that can make the other person uncomfortable. But that wasn't serving the person I wanted to be. And it was costing me my peace and relationships to not be honest about how I felt or how I wanted to be treated.

Platonic Relationships

I am a community-oriented person. I love creating and holding space for others to be seen and heard. During the pandemic, this looked like hosting brunches at my house. I would open a group chat with my favorite people, let them know it was time for some quality time, and propose a few dates. Picture an exchange of emojis and twerking memes. (Cringe? Maybe. But very on brand for summer 2020.) By the end of the chat, we had a plan for our shenanigans. I would remind my friends to come empty-handed and ready to have fun. All I asked was for everyone to be on time because the food was going to be prepared fresh.

Now, I should mention the ethnicities of my friend group to truly set the expectation and reality of what happened. Have you heard of CPT? It's known as Colored People Time and is used as the reason for all late arrivals by Black and Brown people requested to be on time to *any* social gathering. Here's how it works: the host sets an event and says the event begins ninety minutes ahead of the *actual* start time to get the group to be punctual. In other words, the time provided is just a suggestion. It's the time you plan to start setting up the tables, chairs, decorations, and bringing out the speakers. It's *not* the time you want your guests to arrive.

So, when the event date and time arrived, my homegirls showed up forty, sixty, and ninety minutes after the time we'd all agreed on. My feelings were hurt. I hated waiting on people (a direct result of my trauma) and when people didn't do what they said they were going to do. (Why did everyone say the time was good?) But I never said anything. I just greeted them as if they were on time.

After a few more brunches like this, I developed resentment toward the people I loved the most. However, it was not them. It was me. It was my fear of rocking the boat.

Romantic Relationships

Unlike my friends, I had no problem stating my desires, needs, and wants in romantic relationships. If my partner picked me up late for dinner, I would immediately communicate my disappointment and desire for timeliness, without even thinking twice about it. My lack of hesitation in expressing my feelings in platonic versus romantic relationships was night and day.

I believed the notion that our partner was supposed to be with us through anything, so we have the right to speak freely about what we want and need. However, I didn't believe the same thing to be true in platonic relationships. Why was that? When did direct and open communication become restricted to romantic relationships?

As I sat with those questions, I started to realize how hypocritical it was of me to have different standards for different relationships.

Not only that, but the double standard was becoming exhausting. I was trying to stand on business and be my truest self in romantic relationships, yet any level of conflict in platonic relationships made me sweat! (Literally.)

Once I started seeing that my fear of conflict was stopping me from experiencing deeper relationships, another situation came up. This time, it was in the hardest area of them all—family. (Be careful what you tell God you want for your life because He will certainly give you a test for your testimony.)

Familial Relationships

I come from a "what goes on in this house, stays in this house" type of family. Which is ironic because I also come from a "we don't talk about that" kind of family. So, silencing my emotions was a learned skill, but I finally broke the cycle during Thanksgiving 2023.

I was back in Southwest Florida, gallivanting with Grammy, my paternal grandma. I needed some hair products, so we stopped at a CVS. As we were checking out, the cashier asked if I needed a plastic bag. This caught me off guard because the West Coast had banned plastic bags. Convenience stores expect you to bring your own reusable bag, pay for a paper bag, or walk out with the items in your hand. It was two items, so I quickly said, "Oh. No, thank you." As the cashier handed me my items, Grammy interjected. "Yes, she does!" and then gave the items back for the cashier to place in the bag. I turned and looked at her in confusion.

"No. I don't."

"Yes. You do. You don't want them thinking you stole something."

I looked to the left. We were three steps from the front door.

"*No* one is thinking that," I replied.

"No bag, please," I gestured to the cashier.

The cashier looked at us both, respected her elders, and handed me a bag.

We walked out the store in silence. When we got in the car, Grammy started talking to me as if nothing had happened. (Girl. Be so for real!) I was fuming in the passenger seat. I thought, *Why would she talk over me? Why did she, as a grown woman to another grown woman, speak for me as if my words didn't have agency?* I was shocked! But my mind wouldn't rest. I kept thinking, *Ohh, I didn't like that.* I was hesitant to say anything because I was raised in a Black household; you don't question your elders. But I couldn't shake the urge to speak.

I was a few years deep into therapy and six months into my boundary work. Both required daily acknowledgement of emotions and expression in safe spaces. I was learning to listen to my emotions and give them the voice they had always had, no matter how uncomfortable it felt.

But at that moment, I sat quietly. And it triggered me. It brought me back to that parent-child dynamic of "Whatever I say goes," or "I know best." It brought me back to an outdated cultural expectation to "not question an adult" or "stay in a child's place." As a child, I could understand the protective mechanism. However, I was in my late twenties, and this dynamic was no longer needed.

I expressed to Grammy my version of the event as well as my disappointment. I acknowledged her concern and highlighted what a continuation of that dynamic looked and felt like for me. I explained that being stripped of my agency and voice could have negative long-term effects. Then I reminded her of her own saying to my late grandpa: "She is not a baby anymore. You have to let her grow up and make her own decisions." She nodded her head and said, "Okay. I'm sorry." I was shocked! I expected some pushback. Instead, I was met with emotional safety—a moment where I could be honest, vulnerable, and accepted as an adult. Suddenly, my jaw unclenched, my tongue moved away from the roof of my mouth, and my body settled deeper into the passenger seat. I was okay.

This moment was proof that my fear of perception amongst my family and friends was hindering me from getting the care I deeply required. I avoided certain conversations about how I felt because I was scared of the end results of those conversations. However, my needs didn't change because my fears of talking about my emotions with certain people did. I learned I had to be honest with myself and others to have my needs acknowledged and met.

After making headway with my family, friends, and partner, I shared my experiences with Amina. She looked at me with warmth in her eyes, and with a smile on her face, she said,

"It's the idea that there are no special relationships."

That regardless of gender or relationship type, everyone should be held to the same standards.

I agreed. If I knew that men wasting my time, and money, while negatively impacting my emotional well-being, was not good for me, then the statement had to be true for women as well. There were no special relationships. Wrong was wrong.

This affirmation changed the way I moved through life. It taught me the true meaning of boundaries. It's not a word to control people but a daily practice to set a standard for myself. It is a way to hold myself accountable for who I say I am and what I say I want. It's not a performance metric for my friends, family, or partner; it's a personal choice that I practice over and over again. And it's not easy.

I know some people say that things get easier with time. I've learned that things get easier with *evidence*. When you have a favorable experience to draw from, it makes it easier to make that decision again. If you have evidence that tells you that this is a safe route, it builds your confidence in your methodology. This is how our brain is rewired after trauma.

Having multiple experiences where I could express the fullness of my emotions and be met with safety and care gave me confidence. It assured me that I could keep expressing my boundaries in a loving way *and* they would be met without contention. It confirmed that similar boundaries could exist across different types of relationships. Whether you are my dad, grandma, best friend, partner, or employer, I am always going to feel hurt when a boundary is crossed. The difference, I learned, was whether I had the confidence to tell each person how I felt.

Getting to this point started with honesty. It started with communicating how I felt instead of letting resentment build up inside of me. Once I did this, I was able to be and live more authentically.

If you are feeling that your friend, family, partner, or boss is being inconsiderate of your time, talents, or opinion, consider that they don't know better because you haven't told them.

Affirmation: There are no special relationships.

Application: Draw back to this affirmation when you feel you are holding onto resentment in your relationships. Use it to remain rooted in the fact that people are just people. We don't need to create special requirements for every kind of person in our lives. We honor ourselves and others by having a standard. We free ourselves of resentment when we define for ourselves what our standards are, what meeting them looks like for others, and how we best receive information if they cannot be met.

Exploration:
1. Are you holding onto resentment in any of your relationships?
   a. If yes, write down what happened and how you both felt. Every detail. A full play-by-play. This helps you look objectively at the actions and the emotions. These need to be separated to have healthy, actionable conversations.
2. What unfavorable interaction(s) took place?
3. Did you communicate your experience?
   a. Communicating discomfort more than once prevents passive-aggressive behavior. No one can remember all of our hurts if mentioned once. Even if it was a conversation with big emotions and consequences. Apply grace.
4. Have you had a similar experience before?
   a. If so, how did you handle the previous conversation?
   b. Was it easier to say how you felt?
      i. If so, why?
      ii. If not, draw back to what you need.
   c. What makes this relationship different?

* * *

Respect yourself enough to stand on it.

SARAH JAKES ROBERTS

Sometimes, we want to be loved so deeply that we fail to ask ourselves what it's costing us to maintain the relationship. What are we willing to endure to keep someone around? What are we willing to sacrifice—in time, money, or peace—to feel chosen? Usually, it's too much. And after going through trials, we are reminded that we deserve more than what we are receiving.

I learned this lesson the hard way. When my platonic relationship turned romantic, I thought, *This is so unexpected, but it's organic. Could this be something real?* (Spoiler: it wasn't, but it's funny how we try to make something out of nothing. Even if it is costing us our mental health and well-being.)

I met Bryce in the summer of 2020. His business partner was pulling together organizations for their video series, and our startup caught his attention. After a few calls between our teammates, Bryce and I were introduced.

We got to know each other on a professional and personal level over two years. Every few months, we hopped on Google Meets and shared our work experiences, newfound hobbies, and future goals. In between business updates, we yapped about being raised in the South, attending schools in Florida, and the stark difference between living on the West Coast and living on the East Coast.

He was a solid business connection.

Then one day, he mentioned he was coming to the Bay Area and wanted to "crash at my place." I didn't feel comfortable with that, so I told him that I already had a friend staying with me. He assured me it wasn't a problem and affirmed he still wanted to meet up. I didn't hear from Bryce that week. Or for the next six months. When he finally reached out, he said he had never made the trip, but he was coming in a few weeks. I told him that I would be busy with work, but I'd message him if my schedule opened up.

It did.

Meeting people for the first time post-pandemic was trippy. Bryce was someone I had shared my fears and dreams with over an extended period, but I had no idea what he was like in 3D. I felt as if I was in *The Twilight Zone*.

We agreed to meet at Portal, one of my favorite brunch spots in Oakland. They had a chilled ambiance, great food, and bottomless drinks. I thought it was perfect. He was coming from another event, so he decided to meet me there. However, I wasn't expecting what happened next. I walked into the packed restaurant, looking at every table for a familiar face. But I didn't see one. Then, a tall, dark, and handsome man signaled for me to come over. Suddenly, my knees went weak. I began to wonder, *Was Bryce always this fine? Sheesh!* I sat down, and we chatted for hours. The conversation was effortless and amusing. I was surprised that the chemistry we had online translated in person.

After we'd finished eating, he told me he was only in town for a few more hours, so I offered to show him some places only a local would know. Then I invited him to an adult field day I was going to. He accepted my offer. We went to my favorite lookout points in Berkeley, then stopped at my house before going to our final destination.

However, we never made it to the field day. When we walked in, he complimented me on my interior design skills and asked for a tour. As we sat on my patio, enjoying the fresh air, he told me he had feelings for me and insinuated that I knew. Dumbfounded, I said, "For me?" He laughed. I had no idea. Our conversations were strictly business. Until they weren't.

One thing led to the next, and the next thing led to our very platonic relationship being romantic. We spent the rest of the night together. Girl, you couldn't tell anybody that was on the outside looking in that we didn't go together, *real bad.*

The next morning, we had the infamous "What are we?" conversation. He expressed interest in me again and invited me to spend his birthday with him the following month. I was shocked by the pace things were moving, but I accepted because he was a breath of fresh air. I felt comfortable around him. (Please put my clown mask on gently.)

Over the next few days, we joked about his visit and secret intentions over texts. I kept thinking about how I had missed the signs that he was interested in me. I was truly shocked. I even had a debrief with my best friends to make sure I wasn't tripping.

After some self-soothing techniques, I thought, *Okay, Ja'Mara. Let's not self-sabotage and get back into dating. Since he is always making the effort to visit me, maybe I should invite him to my Palm Springs trip in a few weeks.* It was less than an hour from his house and would give us more time to connect before his birthday. He liked the idea and said he'd let me know within the week, once he had a better idea of his schedule.

The following week, he called me saying, "I think you're moving too fast." (Yeah . . . my jaw was on the floor, too.) I thought, *This can't be the same man who was pursuing me, making plans to see me, and expressing unspoken feelings now saying I was moving too fast. This has to be a joke.* It wasn't. It was very real, and so was the confusion and pain.

When you spend years in therapy, especially healing from manipulative relationships, finding yourself in another one hurts. Actually, it's disheartening. You start wondering, *How did this happen? Again? I did things differently. Yet I ended up with the same results.*

That was only partially true. I had done things differently, but the results weren't the same. For the first time in my life, I reacted differently. Normally, I would be desperate for clarity and closure. I would cling to the idea that a conversation would fix everything, so I'd send texts or voice notes apologizing for the "misunderstanding" while simultaneously trying to justify my actions. But not this time. This was the first time I let actions speak louder than words. I didn't go back and forth. I didn't overexplain. Instead, I let their absence be the closure. I vowed to stop begging for clarity when the other person had no interest in providing it.

It wasn't easy doing something I'd never done. For the next month, I ruminated over every conversation we'd had—in my mind, in my journal, and with my therapist. I tried to insert answers where there were none. Was I asking for too much? Was I doing too much? He showed interest in me, but if I showed it back, it's wrong? I started doubting myself.

And because I'd told my best friends about him, I was completely embarrassed. I thought, *This is the person I praised? The man who ghosted me? Girl, what? Wait. Am I doing what I always do? Did I get invested too early? Nah. It's been two years. It wasn't early. It was a slow burn, right?* My doubts moved to shame, a deep-rooted embarrassment after realizing my foolish behavior. But I couldn't hold my own shame or let anyone see it.

So, I isolated myself. I started trying to control what I could: my actions. I worked out daily, returned to the Word, and completed my three-month goals in four weeks. I, by all accounts, slipped into depression and told my friends that I'd got so much done because I'd "focused on myself." In theory, yes. In reality, I exhausted my mind and body because I couldn't control what was beyond my control. My anger turned inward, and I was battling myself.

This carried on for a few months. But I regained my confidence and peace of mind with the support of my friends, faith, and therapist. I reentered the world with a fresh perspective and attitude. But that didn't last long.

That November, I went to my first tech conference in Austin, TX. On the first night, I was looking for my homegirl in a crowded venue when I ran into Bryce. Some would call it fate, but I called it the ultimate test. One that I failed with flying colors. One thing led to another, and *somehow* I spent the rest of the weekend hanging out with him. (Please hand me my clown mask back.) When the conference ended, he ghosted me—like clockwork.

A few weeks later, he messaged me. I scoffed. "Why are you on my line?" He said he really wanted to apologize. His message was sincere—for the first time in a long time. So, I entertained a call. He apologized profusely and asked if he could make it up to me. He had recently moved back East and invited me for my birthday. Now, I wish I could tell you I didn't fall for it. But I did. (Yeah . . . slowly slides down the wall.) I thought, *Okay! He's finally being serious and intentional.* He wasn't.

After seeing the same pattern over and over, I had to get real with myself. I had to call a spade a spade and see the situation for what it was. He wasn't looking for love, growth, or anything meaningful. He just wanted someone to fill his time with. Nothing more. Nothing less.

By allowing him to come in and out of my life, I was showing that I was willing to endure anything for his time and attention. And that made me angry. My own behavior made me resentful. I didn't have a boundary or respect for myself. That was hard to sit with. But it was my honest truth.

It wasn't a truth I got to on my own. Between therapy with Amina and late-night conversations with my best friends, I watched a sermon by Sarah Jakes Roberts. I was looking for anything to pull me out of my isolation and shame. Sarah was preaching about change when she looked at the audience and said,

"Respect yourself enough to stand on it!"

My eyes got wide. I don't know how the Holy Ghost came from a pre-recorded YouTube video to my one-bedroom apartment in Oakland, California, but He was on my doorstep, speaking to me personally.

In the moments when I wanted to reach out, explain the miscommunications, and make everything as it was before, I kept hearing "Respect yourself enough to stand on it" in the back of my mind—and sometimes in the front.

While it's difficult breaking your own patterns, it's even more difficult to do the same thing over and over and over, thinking that something is going to change. Actually, it's textbook insanity. So, you have to fight the internal war within yourself to soothe others who did you wrong. Traditionally, you learn this habit as a child. An authoritative figure could be wrong, but you are conditioned to apologize first and forgive them. What it actually does is remove accountability from its true owner. (Who knew?) Give it back. Let *them* speak to and for their own actions.

If you are no longer getting what you want or need from someone, respect yourself enough to gracefully walk away. No apology. No explanation. You never needed two people to heal anyways.

Affirmation: Respect yourself enough to stand on it.

Application: Draw back to this affirmation when you need a reminder that you can do hard things in relationships. Use it to remain rooted in the fact it takes time, discipline, and consistency to break patterns, but you are more than capable. Whatever you are going through right now is not worth losing your dignity over. So, stand up for yourself, gracefully. Make the hard decision and know it's going to be okay. If not in this moment, then in the next.

Exploration:
1. When was the last time you felt disrespected?
2. What actions led to the situation?
3. What tough decisions did you or do you have to make?
4. What would you gain financially, mentally, physically, or emotionally by making those decisions?
5. In the long run, would you feel better or worse? Be honest. It's just you right now.
6. Is it more important for you to keep the things you're losing or receive the things you are gaining?
   a. If the losses are important, stay the course.
   b. If the gains are more important, respect yourself enough to stand on it.

How Do I Overcome Resentment?

Resentment isn't a flaw. It's feedback. It tells you where something is off and what needs attending to. It tells you that you've stayed silent for too long and that silence is costing you more than it's protecting. It's your invitation to choose clarity over confusion, peace over pleasing, truth over tension. That choice might feel scary and may change your relationships, but it will set you free from the hold your silence has over you.

Resentment is an accumulation of anger, silence, unmet expectations, and giving more than you receive. It's what happens when you overextend yourself and want acknowledgement, praise, or appreciation but it never comes. Likely because you never told them.

You overcome resentment when you realize it's not about what others do. It's about what you don't say. The other person is not a mind reader. Take the pressure off of them to accommodate all your unspoken needs. Communicate clearly, set boundaries early, and remember that no relationship is so special that it exempts someone from respecting your values.

It's time to finally say what you need with honesty, grace, and oomph!

(Now, hold my hand.)

You are more than capable.

seven

OVERCOMING GRIEF

when you feel you don't have a way through

Underneath resentment is grief—for what didn't happen, who didn't show up, and why you didn't notice sooner. It is the heavy truth that something meaningful has been broken, changed, or left behind.

It's an emotion that can lurk in the background for weeks, months, and even years, only rearing its head during your seasons of growth, comfort, or turbulence. Showing off the depth of your pain during seemingly unrelated events.

One moment, you are doing fine. Then, you lose your job. Now, you are overwhelmed with a sadness that you feel you have been carrying for years. To push aside the unexpected emotion, you take a deep breath, think of all you have to be grateful for, and carry on as if nothing happened. You carry on as if everything is okay. But it's not. And you don't know why. You think, "It's just a job." But really it's years of not feeling financially secure, or respected by your peers, or confident that there is more out there for you.

You're not grieving one thing. You're grieving every insecurity and past version of yourself.

I get it. I am no stranger to grief. Actually, there are some seasons where we are best friends. I learned the way to move with grief is to stop trying to "carry on" as though it no longer exists. It does, and to some degree, always will. I found that sitting with the loss or separation is the way through.

Whenever you feel you'll never recover from grief, lean on these affirmations to remind you that love doesn't need a recovery plan.

* * *

I can absorb the loss.

MARIANNE WILLIAMSON

In 2024, I changed my life for the fourth time. (Apparently, once wasn't enough.) I decided I wanted to move back East and start over. New city. New mindset. New life. Everything was changing, and I was ready to change too.

I had built a strong community on the West Coast, but I was feeling disconnected from them. If I'm honest, I was feeling disconnected from myself. I thought, *Who am I without the crutch of my community? Who do I want to be? Could I be that person somewhere else? Alone?* I didn't have all the answers, but I wanted to find out. I had faith that moving would make me feel alive, present, and connected again.

As I started to plan my cross-country journey, I kept getting the go-ahead to move forward. I didn't have any issues with work, housing, or movers. I thought, *Is God giving me the alley-oop to live my dreams?*

I told my therapist how surprisingly everything was working out. She wasn't surprised. She knew it would. She explained how divine forces provide compensation and support when we align ourselves with our higher purpose. She had read about it in *The Law of Divine Compensation* by Marianne Williamson. After our session, she invited me to read it as well.

The next week, I listened to it on Audible.

Girl, let's just say that I wasn't ready for the hard truth Marianne was going to give me at 7:32 in the morning. I was lying in bed, listening to Marianne describe her first big, and expensive, event as an entrepreneur. She expected hundreds of people to attend, but fewer than a hundred came. When she talked with her dad about the disappointing event, he reminded her that it was a perfect event. The people who were supposed to be there were there. It was intimate, she made new contacts that helped her business, and her attendees gave her positive reviews. As she thought about her expectations and the borrowed money she had lost, her father reminded her that she could absorb the loss.

"I can absorb the loss,"

she repeated. Meaning she was blessed enough to put on an event where she could cover all her expenses, even if the return on her investment wasn't immediate or as expected.

(Record scratch.)

I pressed pause on the remote. I stared at the TV screen, and the screen stared back at me. Then, I looked around the room to make sure I wasn't the only one who had heard that message. (I was. I lived alone.) "Marianne, are you seeing me when I don't want to be seen? Alright now, Miss Girl," I blurted.

Her words struck a chord with me. So much was changing that as I prayed for what I could gain, I couldn't help but dwell on what I would lose. *Who* I would lose. While I knew that loss was on the way, nothing could have prepared me for the change that was coming.

From my mid-twenties to early-thirties, I was in a back-and-forth relationship with Aaron. We would date for a few months, realize we wanted different things, and then break up. Only to be stuck like glue to each other again for comfort and proximity. Our titles changed, but the love and care did not. This often left our friends questioning whether we were still together. We weren't, but it always looked as if we were.

I got used to our complicated dynamic. Through the chaos of love, growth, and unpleasant endings, we supported each other through every milestone: new jobs, new situationships, family drama, friend drama, death, etc. We were each other's confidant, travel partner, and overall favorite person. That was us. For almost a decade, *he* was my home away from home. I never saw that changing.

Then I moved 3,000 miles away. The love was still there, but the proximity was gone. And after six months, he decided to enter a new relationship.

Girl, cut the cameras to me crying like a girl on *The Maury Show* who just found out that the man she'd told the audience was 100 percent the baby's father, well, was not. Now she's screaming and falling on the floor with a perfectly positioned camera in front of her face. (Yeah, that's how I see myself during difficult seasons.

A frantic woman on *Maury* who's been told her expectations and beliefs were a lie.)

After the tears came anger and confusion. I started to question my decision-making. How could I invest so much and have nothing to show for it? Did I really become *that* girl who spends years with a guy who is committed to decommitting? Then I started to question Aaron's decisions. How could he willingly give the level of commitment and certainty I had asked for over eight years to someone he was unsure of after one month of dating? (Okay, add in feelings of rejection, too.)

I was *so* embarrassed. I felt as though I had wasted my time and everybody knew it. As if, on the outside looking in, my friends were saying, "I told you so." I didn't have a ring, a house, or a child to show for my multi-year investment. Not to say all those things were on my wish list, but our ending was completely unexpected.

More than anything, I felt betrayed. While we had talked to other people in the past, we never made it official with anyone else. While I knew he was dating, I was completely blindsided about how he *actually* felt about her or what his intentions were with her. The lack of honesty and transparency left me at a loss for words. I realized that my closest relationship—my home—was a complete loss.

I was lost—for weeks. I couldn't wrap my mind around what and who I had lost. Then one day, as I was ugly crying on my bedroom floor at 2:30 a.m.—exactly six months into the new life I had begged God for—I remembered "I can absorb the loss." I remembered that while it felt like a loss, if I shifted my perspective, I would be able to see what I had gained—just as Marianne did.

I had some of the best experiences of my life with my ex. I learned things about myself, my career, and my finances that only came to light *because* of our proximity. I traveled to places I had never thought about because he was the ideal travel partner and planner. And I learned what it meant to do life with someone during its difficult stages: supporting someone through a job promotion when you have nothing to gain, learning what to say or do when someone loses a parent, or how to have healthy discourse when you can't see eye to eye. I learned all these things by doing life with him.

While the end of the relationship was unexpected, so were all the experiences along the way. I had never dreamed of a West Coast lifestyle, but I built one because of him. Those eight years of my life were possible because I saw that relationship through. Our relationship served us both—until it couldn't.

When I let the weight of that truth sit, I realized that I could absorb the loss, too. Why? Because it wasn't a loss. I hadn't lost anything by being active and present in my life. I had only gained perspective, community, experiences, communication, love, and freedom. It was mine to gain, all along.

This is your truth, too.

The very thing you believe will take you out emotionally, financially, spiritually, or physically might also be the very thing that's saving you. The person, experience, or job that you are grieving over might be the catalyst for your growth. It might be the lesson or skill you finally needed to learn to get to your next level. Or the mental shift you needed to chase your dreams and not people.

While it may have been hard to separate from the person, there were positives that came from it. Despite the loss, you may have gained money, skills, or a fresh perspective. You may have met people you never would have met otherwise. Although the situation may not be what you had hoped, or even prayed for, it doesn't mean you can't absorb the "loss" too.

Affirmation: You can absorb the loss.

Application: Draw back to this affirmation whenever your reality is not meeting your expectations. Give yourself permission to be wrong about the way you thought it was going to go. Give yourself permission to update yourself on your new reality. The results may be different, but they may also be better.

Exploration:
1. What didn't go to plan?
2. What were you expecting?
3. What happened in its place?
4. Is there anything that you wish had happened? Pause to think about that.
5. What skills are you learning or unlearning as you navigate this transition?
6. What I-can-not-believe-this-is-happening experience do you want to have for your praise report instead of your prayer report?

* * *

Recovery is living with unfinished business.

THERAPIST

Ever had a relationship end that you didn't want to end? Or should I say you had a relationship end that you didn't have a say in *how* it ended? Two people in the relationship, but you didn't have a say in what happened next.

Now, y'all have been down for years, through thick and thin, hell and high water, the good, the bad, and the ugly. Truly two peas in a pod.

Then one day, you're not.

One day, you're the only pea in the pod.

One day, you have to explain to your friends and family that y'all are no longer together.

That they are no longer around.

You can't explain it, and it wasn't your choice. You just know that you are grieving the relationship you once had. One minute you're laughing and reminiscing on the phone with your parents, and the next you're crying in the grocery store parking lot. (Now, this is my testimony, so insert your own awkward, but very public, location.)

That was me when I found out my grandpa, one of my primary caretakers, had passed away.

As true as the saying goes, it takes a village to raise a child. My grandpa was my anchor. Although he was in and out of the hospital for the last two years of his life, I never imagined or planned for his death. Nor did I ever want to. But it wasn't my choice. Death knocked on my door.

Soon after, I realized I was dealing with a level of pain that was *well* beyond my pay grade. I didn't know what to do. So I was doing everything under the sun. It was summer, but I was acting as if it was a "college summer." I was staying out late on weekdays to go to happy hours, house parties, and game nights. Doing any and every event you can imagine to avoid being alone—to avoid *feeling* alone. I was faking it until I made it, but I wasn't making it. I was only a shell of myself: physically here, but not mentally present.

Three months passed before I sought a therapist. (Yes, the same Amina you've seen throughout these pages.) In our first meeting, I told her what I wanted to work on, what my limiting beliefs were, and what I wanted to get out of the journey. I was grief-stricken and wanted to get unstuck. I had a limiting belief that I wasn't good at relationships and wanted to see how my experiences and traumas were playing a role in how I showed up in them. Ultimately, I wanted to feel happy, empowered, and enlightened about my traumas, decisions, and inspirations.

Since I had a lot of heavy emotions, Amina started with grief. I told her about how I found out about my grandpa's passing. It was 7:00 a.m., I had just finished my 5:00 a.m. workout with my coworkers, and I was headed to the office. I was feeling *so* good that I said, "This is such a good day!" Minutes later, my grandma called me to tell me Grandpa was not going to make it. Hours later, while I was mid-flight back to Florida, he passed.

As we unpacked that moment, I realized I had formed a belief that day. I believed that claiming good days triggered my worst days. So my therapist asked me to unpack that belief; she really called my grief to the front stage. (She still has a knack for doing that. Making me feel seen by calling my inner child forward to share the emotions I have been strategically suppressing.)

I explained that I was disappointed, no, devastated about the moments I would never have with him. Moments I always planned to experience, such as him walking me down the aisle, becoming a great-grandpa, or riding around town with me to buy stuff I didn't need from the department store. I was sad about all the moments we'd had and would never have again. The Sunday calls to ask about the weather that he had clearly already seen on the news. The grocery store runs where he would talk to a random person as though he had known them all his life; after they'd left, I'd ask, "Where do you know them from?" and he would say, "Oh, I don't know them," in a matter-of-fact tone. The support and encouragement to "stay away from those boys" as we sat on the back patio, chatting about my life in college or California. The many life lessons that would include him as a critical part of my strategy team and emotional safety blanket. I was sad about all the things that had never occurred and could never occur now. The hardest part, I couldn't even tell him.

After hearing all this, my therapist said in her calming and reassuring voice,

"Yes. Recovery is living with unfinished business."

Girl, I had only known her for twenty minutes, yet I was boo-hoo crying in her dimly lit office. She was right. I had to get comfortable releasing control of how I thought and wanted life to go. I didn't have a choice. Not in how, or *when*, the relationship ended. God didn't consult me. No matter how much I questioned Him. But I soon learned it was in His perfect timing.

You see, my grandfather passed away in April 2019.

In October 2018, six months before, my roommate mentioned she was moving out of California, so I went back home for three months to figure out my life. During that time, I helped my grandma take care of my grandpa. His health was declining rapidly, and he needed constant care. The responsibilities were weighing my grandma down emotionally and physically. (You never know what someone is going through until you live it.)

As I stepped in, I learned what it is truly like to be a caregiver of an aging adult. I understood what it truly means to love someone in sickness and in health. It's the hardest and most exhausting job you could have, but much like parenthood, you do it with a willing and eager heart because you love them.

Since I was working remotely, grandpa and I had three months of quality time together. We shared space, laughter, and sometimes, tears. More importantly, we shared our love for each other, always reminding each other that I was still his "baby" and he was still my "grampy wampy."

Less than a year after his passing, Covid hit. I often think about this divine timing. If Grandpa had lived to 2020, he would have likely contracted the virus in the hospital, since that was becoming more his home than his actual home. Which means he would have been isolated, and we would not have been able to see him in his final hours. And our family would have been among the statistics of loved ones who lost someone to an unforgiving virus. But that wasn't God's plan. It wasn't a part of His timing. Back then, I couldn't understand. Now, I do. I am grateful for Grandpa's final months, specifically that I was able to share them with him, as God intended.

It took me a year before I could get rid of that belief and claim a day as "good." Even if everything about the day made me happy, I couldn't claim it. I learned to accept that life would have many more twists and turns, and just because things didn't ultimately turn out the way I wanted, that didn't make the whole thing bad. The same way a relationship may end, but it doesn't make the other person bad. The same way a job may end, but it doesn't make the role or the company bad. Not to say that this is never the case, but it's not the standard.

You decide what you want to do with your unfinished business. And you get to decide how you want to recover—in agony or in peace. I hope you choose peace. I hope you allow others to see you. Let them witness your humanity and support your new reality. That is how you recover. When you share your unfulfilled dreams—an international trip, a bestselling book, a new business, a new home, or even a partner—you invite others to help you *finish* your business. Allow it. Without question. Without reason. Allow it.

Affirmation: Recovery is living with unfinished business.

Application: Draw back to this affirmation when you don't get the ending you wanted. Use it to remain rooted in the fact that healing is a journey. Grief is a journey. Each of those journeys is a solo one, but there are people who can point you in the right direction or be an ear when you need to process your emotions. Grief is not linear; one minute you think you're fine, and the next you're not. It's okay. It's normal. You're normal. It's all a part of living.

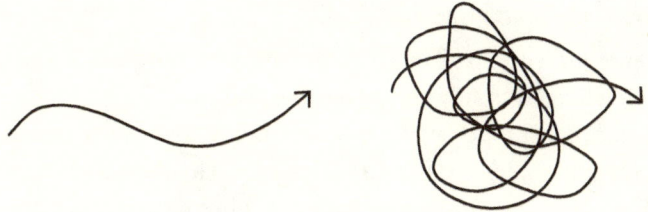

Figure 4: Grief Expectation vs Reality

Exploration:
1. What are you experiencing that keeps you feeling "stuck" in the past?
    a. Is it something you wish you could say, but never did?
    b. Is it something you did, but wish you hadn't?
2. How long have you been holding onto this feeling?
3. What would it look like to live, as best as you can, with your unfinished business in peace?
4. What would it look like to live without an apology from or explanation to the other person?
5. Can you forgive without forgetting?
    a. Have you ever been forgiven without someone forgetting?
    b. Can you apply that same grace to them? If not, that's okay. E is for effort, and if that's all you have to give right now, so be it.

How Do I Overcome Grief?

Grief is not supposed to be dealt with or overcome. It should be acknowledged, held, and cared for. It is your indicator that you still care for the person or have feelings about the situation. It is your signal that you can still feel deeply. That's great. That means you are alive. Even when you are not thinking about it, your body is reminding you that you are alive.

You acknowledge your grief with care when you identify the tell-tale signs that you are grieving. Are you doing things you don't normally do? Are you all of a sudden feeling sad when everything around you should make you happy? Are you sulking over memories instead of embracing your new reality? Get honest with yourself about how you feel and how you are coping.

You hold your grief when you don't try to rush past your emotions. When you make time to be present through the stages of grief: denial, anger, bargaining, depression, and acceptance. And when you allow yourself to move through the stages freely (because people tend to go back and forth) and without a timeframe (because grief can't tell time).

You care for your grief when you accept that whatever happened to you happened *for* you. While it may be hard, it is not over. You can absorb the loss. And with time, you will learn to *live* with the unfinished business instead of "pushing through" or "taking it day by day."

(Now, hold my hand.)

You're okay. *You* are the way through.

eight

OVERCOMING HOPELESSNESS

when you feel everything is pointless

Emotions have a tendency to build. What can start as one thing can easily transform into three or four more things. Unprocessed doubt, fear, or anxiety can become hopelessness. Similarly, unresolved grief or prolonged loss of control can turn into the same emotion.

While the paths to hopelessness may be different, the signs are the same. Something happens, such as rejection from a job or separation from a person. You brush it off, thinking it wasn't meant to be and something better is waiting for you. But you don't stop thinking about it. You try to occupy your time with other things, but it doesn't work. So you try something else, but the same thing happens. Your peace takes a hit.

You start to lose interest in things that once brought you joy. You think it's seasonal. A loss of your creative spark or temporary identity shift, but then you find yourself isolated from the people you love. You wonder if your social battery is running low and you need some time to recharge, but then you notice a persistent sadness hovering over you. Now, you're irritated at everyone and everything. You don't know why. Nor do you mean to be. But you are. And it feels as if you are drowning with no one to help. You're embarrassed to feel this way, so you sink deeper into depression. And as your new reality settles, you start feeling hopeless. As if nothing will ever change.

I get it. I like to lead, plan, and be certain, too—of people and outcomes. So, when multiple things I didn't plan for happen, I feel defeated. But I learned that the plan is just a plan; it is not the law. Things can change, and they likely will. However, a changed plan does not determine my preparedness or value. I do.

Whenever you feel hopelessness trying to make itself at home, lean on these affirmations to remind you that change will come, and it will be in your favor.

* * *

Things not working out is a blessing too.

UNKNOWN

If I could go back and tell my twenty-year-old self anything, it would be: get comfortable with endings. Nothing is as permanent as you want it to be because everything is evolving. You are evolving. Although you may feel deep regret, confusion, or shame about your decisions, your greatest blessings will come on the heels of difficult endings—sometimes on the same day.

When I was in my last semester of college, I realized the degree and career I thought I wanted were no longer a desire of mine. I'd spent all my time and the government's money on a degree I wasn't going to use. (Imagine me telling my low-income family that their first-generation daughter may, or may not, be graduating.)

As I thought about my embarrassing reality, I realized I had two options: finish the health degree and try to move up at my call center job, *or* double major in health and business. Neither option seemed promising. One option felt like a waste of time since I didn't need a college degree to work at the call center. The other option felt like a waste of resources since I didn't have the funds or time to double major. So, I decided to finish my undergrad in health and get a master's in business. I figured that decision would give me more time to figure out what was next. Because I needed it.

As I looked into graduate programs, my first choice was my soon-to-be alma mater. However, when I told them my situation, they said, "Yeah, no." I didn't have the prerequisites as a health major, and the school no longer offered the MBA program for non-business majors. How ironic. So, my only option to attend my alma mater was to finish my undergrad degree and take *another* semester of prerequisites to qualify for the following year's incoming class. That was time, money, and patience I didn't have.

That crushed me. Then, the admission counselor graciously told me to check out their competitor because they were number one in the state and offered a program that fit my needs. (Girl, sometimes rejection is redirection.)

I had little expectation of getting into that graduate program. I had an average GPA and a "needs improvement" GMAT score. However, I always had a warrior spirit and the faith of a mustard seed. I thought, *Let's just see*, as I filled out my application and attended their introductory meetings.

While some of my application details did not stand out, my essay and visibility got me in the room for an interview. And when the day came to tell them why I deserved a spot in the upcoming class, I was excited, but also *really* nervous. I knew I did great things and could handle it, but would they think the same? I didn't know.

But my community did. They praised God as if the acceptance was already mine. They believed it was possible for me, even when the evidence was questionable or non-existent. Their level of faith and spirit of expectation were what carried me into that room. As I waited for the interviewer to call my name, I followed their example. I praised Him in the midst of my wishes and desires.

When I entered the small office for my panel interview, I thought, *You didn't make it this far to make it this far. Let's do this.* I sat down and gave my best answers.

Girl. I ate that interview up! They were impressed and *I* was impressed. I thought, *Did we really just convince a team of business professionals that I'm the crème de la crème? Me? Little ol' me? Yeaaaah-hhh. Hire me for president!*

As I drove back to my call center job, I received an email. It read, "We would like to congratulate you on your acceptance into the early MBA program for Spring."

When I tell you I cried, I cried. I believed it, but I couldn't believe it. The girl who didn't know where her life was heading, or what she was doing eight months prior, secured acceptances to three MBA programs. The girl who was told she did not qualify for her alma mater was told, "You're the one" by a highly respected MBA program. (Or at least that was how I heard it.)

This gave me the confidence that even when I don't know how my dreams are going to come to pass, God is always working in my favor.

It took me years to put language around this moment and its butterfly effect. Then, one day, I was scrolling on social media and saw this quote:

"Things not working out is a blessing too."

I took a deep breath and nodded in agreement. It resonated. I was a testament to changed plans becoming a blessing—more than once.

And here's the truth: so are you.

When things don't work out, we tend to ruminate on the details and motive. We tend to waste time trying to figure out how we can change others' minds, our behaviors, or the end results. We say things like, "Why did this happen? Was it something I said or did? Am I not good enough?"

No. Things not working out is a blessing too. Why? Because God is bigger than the details. The way you imagined it was too small. The way they said was possible was not possible for *you*. God has another way to bless you. Are you open to that? Are you ready for your plan to be thrown in the trash so he can reveal your next level?

He wants to take you from Glory to Glory, but you keep asking Him to make a way for your Level 1 Glory when He is already moving things around for your Level 3 Glory. (Embarrassing? Girl, yes!)

What's for you will never pass you if you get out of the way. If you get comfortable with endings and new beginnings. *If* you remember that things (jobs, relationships, or financial plans) not working out is a blessing too.

Affirmation: Things not working out is a blessing too.

Application: Draw back to this affirmation when you are trying to figure out whether what just happened is a loss or a win. Use it to remain rooted in the fact that rejection can be divine redirection. Don't force it. Find another way to get to your end goal. Don't spend too much time questioning the process. Just decide on a new one that works better for you. Your blessing will never pass you by.

Exploration:
1. When was the last time you felt defeated? What didn't work out in your favor?
2. What did you have to do instead to reach your goal?
3. Would you have thought of that plan had your first plan worked out?
4. What emotions do you feel when you realize that you reached your goals, even if the process took a different turn?
5. What other things in your life didn't "work out" but worked out?
   a. Use them as evidence that you are, in fact, blessed.

* * *

Just because you lost the outlet doesn't mean you lost your purpose.

SARAH J. ROBERTS

When you discover your purpose for being on this earth, you feel unstoppable. Like nothing is standing in your way because the stars have finally aligned for you. Now, life will be easier and more enjoyable because you are on a straight path to your destiny. But what happens when things change? The career that supported your community is now in jeopardy. The house that was going to be a safe haven for your family is now off the market. That partner you were building a family with decides to leave. What happens? Well, if your first answer is "crash out," then you're right! But afterward, your mind is going to trick you into thinking this is the end. That the way you went about fulfilling your purpose was the *only* way it could have happened. But it's not. Here's how I found out.

During the pandemic, I built a startup focused on career accessibility within the underrepresented community. Think Black and Brown people getting career advice in the technology or medical fields. This was a completely new path for me as I had never built a business before, let alone one from scratch. But when my friend Tristan asked me to join his team, I jumped at the opportunity. I was already doing this work with the neighboring community college and saw it as an opportunity to expand. Plus, I would get exposure to new aspects of business, such as sales pricing, product development, and marketing. It became an easy yes.

Everything was great, until it wasn't. Eight months after agreeing to build the startup, I found myself working on two full-time opportunities with tight deadlines. I was burnt out. And it didn't help that my co-founder and I were having communication issues as well. It wasn't the best of times. So, I decided to quit the role. Tristan accepted my decision.

I was crushed. Butt-hurt. Soul-shattered.

Why did he take my resignation so easily? Was I not a good co-founder? Did I no longer have value or use in the organization? If I'm not a founder—an identity I spent months stepping into—then what am I? What purpose do I have? Those questions sat on my heart for months, which felt like years during the pandemic.

But I couldn't shake the impending identity crisis. I became restless in my mind and my body. Then I started becoming irritable because I wasn't sleeping or eating enough. I was dropping weight so fast that my friends were concerned. But I didn't see what they saw: an overwhelmed woman who was barely holding on. Instead, I saw a woman who was chasing her newfound purpose but was unsure whether it was meant to be *truly* hers.

Luckily, my therapist, Amina, got to hear me cry about how I didn't want something, then turn around and cry about how I still wanted it.

I wanted to stay because I enjoyed the work I was doing, the people I was interacting with, and the new identity I was stepping into. A founder? Me? Girl, you have to be kidding me! I'd never thought about starting a company, and now I was stepping into an identity I didn't know could exist.

I wanted to leave because I didn't enjoy always being on. I didn't enjoy going to bed thinking about problems we could solve, how we were going to make money, and how to meet my co-founder's new expectations. I also didn't enjoy how long it was taking us to have difficult conversations. I was exhausted and twenty pounds lighter.

Amina let me sit with the duality of my emotions for a moment. The truth was painfully loud. My mind was telling me to choose a side, but my therapist was telling me there were no sides to choose from. She explained that both emotions were valid. They were honest parts of me that could, and oftentimes did, coexist. That was hard to accept.

A few weeks later, I was soul-searching on YouTube and came across a sermon on purpose by Sarah Jakes Roberts. It felt befitting for my mood, so I watched it.

Girl, let me just say Sarah gets me all the way together every time!

She was discussing how she hadn't thought being a pastor was her story because of what she'd been through and what she'd lost. The path that she thought was for her changed, and she was presented with an option she'd never considered. With conviction in her eyes, she said,

> **"Just because you lost the outlet doesn't mean you lost your purpose."**

Suddenly, everything clicked. I ended up crying on my bedroom floor, grateful for the message I had received about my own life. While I was questioning whether I was still enough to be considered an entrepreneur, she had confirmed that it was just a single outlet. I still held the experiences, skills, and title of an entrepreneur regardless of the organization I was at.

When a founder sells their business, they are forever known as the founder of that company, even if they don't work there anymore. When a mother's child moves out of the house, she is still someone's mother. When a pastor leaves his home congregation, he is still referred to as pastor.

Why did I think it was any different for me? Why did I think that a single outlet had erased my gifts, experience, and purpose? It hadn't. The only thing that had changed was my outlet.

By accepting that outlet was ending, I was able to explore others with confidence. I'd learned how to build from scratch and to bring others along for the journey. Most importantly, I'd learned how to do things that scared me. And to do them with a little oomph, a little joy, and a little courage.

Whenever you are feeling you've lost your purpose or identity, remember that it was never lost. Your purpose is not what you provide but who you are. We all have specific purposes on earth because of the gifts that have been given to us. Your talents and experiences come together to make you the perfect person for the job. Every time. That can never be taken from you.

So, whenever your outlet changes, change with it! Every experience is conspiring to push you toward your divine purpose. Don't take it for granted. Lean into it.

Affirmation: Just because you lost the outlet doesn't mean you lost your purpose.

Application: Draw back to this affirmation when you need a reminder that there is more than one path to your purpose. Use it to remain rooted in the fact that just because it didn't work out how you planned doesn't mean it's not going to work out at all. The vision, desire, and purpose on the inside of you never went away; it just changed over time, as you did. So allow the path to your end goal to change as well.

Exploration:
1. What is your purpose?
   a. Narrow that down to an actionable benefit to others, e.g., build a family, save lives, feed the homeless, build an equitable workplace, or break a generational curse.
2. How do you plan to fulfill that purpose?
3. What other ways can you fulfill your purpose?

    a. If you have trouble thinking of other ways, ask people who share your purpose.
4. Are you comfortable with there being multiple routes to your end goal?
5. Are you comfortable taking an unconventional route?

* * *

Starting from scratch is not the same as starting from experience.

SARAH J. ROBERTS

"We regret to inform you that your loan application has been denied."

"We are unable to offer you a place in the Class of 2026."

"I think you are incredible. I just need to work on myself first."

"We've made the difficult decision to move forward with another candidate."

(Slides down the wall.)

It doesn't matter how many times you see these phrases in your inbox. They never get easier to accept. Rejection, in any form, never gets easier. Innately, you analyze all the things that might have gone wrong and all the ways you could've changed their mind. If they would just give you a chance to explain your qualifications or their misunderstandings (because it's never our misunderstanding), then you could make it right. If you could just talk it through, you could avoid the feelings of devastation, shame, and anger altogether. You could avoid the simple fact that no matter how much you were sure this was the perfect next step in your master plan in life, it wasn't the right avenue, person, or time.

Why are we so obsessed with being right? Because of shame. If that person, employer, school, or bank only knew what it took for you to get here, they would reconsider. If they only knew all the things you have sacrificed, all the people that were rooting for you, all that you have invested, or even all the doors this would open, they wouldn't have rejected you.

But they don't. So, they did what was best for them, which leaves you feeling as though you've taken three steps forward to go ten steps back. It sucks. You're crushed. You're ashamed. How are you going to tell everyone you know that the plan didn't work out? How can you accept that this isn't the way you planned it, the way God may have shown it to you, or the way your community may have helped you set it up? In your mind, this was the only way. Now you have to go back to the drawing board. You have to have a very real conversation with yourself that you are back at ground zero. You are starting from scratch. And as much as it hurts to say it, it's reality.

I'm here to tell you that that is fake news! I've been in this situation more times than not. Quite literally sliding down walls, chairs, and even appliances. From the outside looking in, "it was not meant to be." Yet I found myself crashing out. I was constantly "leveling up" to cope with the fact that I felt unworthy.

One day, mid-crash-out over a failed business venture, I was watching Sarah Jakes Roberts's "The Undoing" sermon on YouTube. I clicked on the video because the title seemed to be mirroring my life: everything was falling apart. As she delivered her message, I was taking notes at lightning speed. Then she turned around, looked deep into the camera, and said,

"Starting from scratch is not the same as starting from experience."

I thought, *What?* It was like she heard me because she repeated the phrase into the camera. I ugly cried like I'd never ugly cried before! She continued to explain that even when God redirects us, we are going back into the process with invaluable experience.

The school that denied you because of your test scores also just gave you the way to improve your next application. The employer that rejected your application for another candidate also just saved you from being in a place where your value may not have been realized. The partner that ended the relationship also just gave you another opportunity to be with someone who is aligned with you.

You can never start from scratch when you are not doing a new thing. This ain't your first rodeo, babe, so why are you letting your emotions lie to you like it is? You've been *here* before! Although you haven't been here with your desired outcome before, you've been here. You know the ways that things can go wrong. Good. That's knowledge. That's experience. Now you can experience ways it can go right! Be open to that. Be available for that. Be curious about it.

Whenever you're feeling rejected, remind yourself of what you learned about the experience, about others, and about yourself during the redirection. Write it down. Now visualize what you can do differently. Visualize the situation going your way. Visualize the experience you had propelling you to the blessing that's on the way.

The spirit of expectancy is real. If you patiently expect your blessing to arrive, it will. When it does, it'll be at the right time and in a big way.

Affirmation: Starting from scratch is not the same as starting from experience.

Application: Draw back to this affirmation when you feel that there was a mistake with the way things turned out. Use it to remain rooted in the fact that there wasn't. Everything went how it was supposed to go. All the emotions you are experiencing are going to be vivid reminders that you have experienced one way things can go, and you are equipped with the tools, resources, and knowledge to make it go another way. Keep chasing your dreams until your dreams are chasing you, too.

Exploration:
1. When was the last time you felt rejected?
2. What did it take you to build up the courage to start that new thing?
3. How did you feel when it didn't work out?
4. What was the reason, given to you or realized through reflections, that it didn't work out?
5. What knowledge does that give you for the next time around?
   a. You can go about it the same way with another employer, vendor, or partner, or you can switch your methods. Both are leaning on your experience.

* * *

What you make happen for others, God will make happen for you.

UNKNOWN

I remember when I finally decided to pursue a fulfilling career—one with upward mobility, great pay, and a flexible schedule. I had to let go of the excuses that I'd held on to for years and step outside my comfort zone. But even after I'd done all of that, I still found myself struggling to obtain the life I wanted. I couldn't go back to throwing myself a pity party, so I stayed the course. I stayed expectant. What I found wasn't a lesson on work ethic or persistence, but faith. I found what could happen when you bring blessings to others while you wait for your own.

I was working in the staffing industry when I got exposed to the project management industry. I saw what my consultants were doing at work and thought, *I have years of experience with this. Why aren't I being hired for these roles?*

As I questioned what made me different from my peers, I realized the only difference was what I was willing to do. Up until that point, I was trying to find a new job while at my old job—my first mistake. My brain, and time, were split between work that drained me and work that fueled me.

I decided enough was enough. I left the staffing industry and went all in on a project management certification. I was changing my identity from a Human Resources Professional to a Project Management Professional. I was finally ready to walk the walk and talk the talk.

Part of that glow-up plan meant updating my resume. Now, working in recruiting, I saw thousands of resume formats. I thought, *I know how to sell my experience and skills. I mean, I work with hiring managers every day.* Turns out I was wrong.

To best showcase my skills, I needed to admit that I needed help. I hired a resume coach who put language to work experiences I thought were irrelevant. She taught me how to highlight actions I'd taken instead of tasks I'd completed with my previous employers. This showed that I knew how to add value to those organizations. It was as if a light switch was turned on. Not only did the interview requests start coming in, but a few months later, I got my first big tech role.

My friends were stunned how I went after the life I wanted. (Sometimes being the example is all you need to do to inspire those around you. It reminds them that they are a mirror of their environment and what can happen for one can happen for all.) They wanted to do it too. It was peak pandemic, and we had nothing but time. I sent an email blast to all my friends and offered to teach them what I had learned from my resume coach.

My homegirl Naomie was experiencing a layoff and wanted to pivot from the education industry to technology. She thought it was impossible because she had never held the title of Creative Project Manager before. I said, "Girl, please! You have so many transferable skills. It just needs a little shaping. I'll help you!" Over the course of forty-eight hours, we transformed her teaching resume into a project manager resume. She was already doing what the industry required; she just wasn't saying it in a language her desired industry understood. A few weeks later, she started getting interview requests. As Naomie's confidence grew, her success rate grew as well. She ended up with a role at Meta, living the life she'd never imagined. God did His big one for her, and I was proud that she was able to experience what she had always deserved.

A few months later, I found myself looking for new opportunities. My contract was coming to an end, and I didn't want to be left without any options, or money, so I implemented the same tools and resources that I'd shared with my friends. I also added some of the tricks they had shown me while they were on the job hunt. For months, it was a mutual exchange of resources. (Love that for us!)

While I was getting interview requests, I wasn't getting offers. I thought, *Am I not on my A-game? Is my current experience too different from what they need?* I started to get worried.

A month later, I got a request from a recruiter about a role I thought was out of my league. Not that I couldn't do it, but I didn't meet any of the job requirements. I thought, *Dang, did the recruiter even read the job description? I'm not technical, nor do I have a degree in engineering. He has the wrong candidate.* I deleted the LinkedIn message. A few days went by, and he reached out again, saying the director had already seen my resume and wanted to interview me as soon as possible. (Girl, when God is working on something, it's best not to question it.) I took the interview and thought nothing of it. Then, after my fourth interview with the team, I realized it was the perfect opportunity for me. It was challenging, exciting, and exactly my area of expertise. I ended up accepting the role I'd thought had been mistakenly sent to me. It was my second big role in the technology industry, but my first full-time opportunity.

Those experiences taught me the importance of investing in my community while I waited for my own blessings to arrive. It taught me the importance of doing the hard work with people closest to me and not just the ones in high places who could give me praise.

It taught me the importance of helping those in my own backyard the same way I helped strangers. More importantly, it taught me the importance of doing all those things out loud instead of in the shadows.

For the first time, I transitioned my career and, ultimately, life, publicly. I brought my friends along with me on my scary journey. I let them see me try new things, and fail at things, and then I let them help me. That changed the game for me.

It allowed those around me to show up in ways I didn't know how to ask for help. For example, when I got the offer for the role I thought I was unqualified for, I had my first experience with negotiations. I was twenty-nine and didn't know anything about salaries, Restricted Stock Units, or 401Ks. Why? Because I had never been offered these benefits by a company before, and none of my family had had any of these benefits before. I was going in blind. But not for long. Because this time, I was building out loud.

So, I told my best friend David, in full transparency, what they were offering me. He was an engineer who had been in tech for years. He had learned the ins and outs of financial stability after growing up in poverty, like me. He was the perfect person to ask for help. He congratulated me and told me what the numbers meant and what I should focus my counteroffer on. With his help, I secured a sign-on bonus (something I'd never had before) and an extra $5,000 in salary. I was living in answered prayers, and I was doing it with the help of my community.

The weekend after accepting my offer, I thought about a quote I'd read on the internet:

> **"What you make happen for others,
> God will make happen for you."**

In other words, the way you give to others will be given to you.

In that season, I wanted to finally step into my purpose and live the life of my dreams. Since I was little, my dream has been to change people's lives or to help them change their circumstances. And while I thought that meant becoming a nurse or a recruiter, I realized there was more than one way to live my purpose. I was doing it just by helping my friends step into theirs. I was living my dream life by showing up week over week with a joyous heart and giving spirit to the ones I loved the most. By stepping away from the transactional work of recruiting, I was able to pour the same skills and lessons I'd learned into my closest friends. I was able to *be* a blessing as I *waited* on my blessing. While I was busy making it happen for others, God was busy making it happen for me. (Can I get an Amen?)

Whenever you feel like the journey is pointless, remember that every experience is being used *for* your purpose. So don't give up. Find another angle, another avenue, or even another journey to go on. And while you are on that journey, look around to see who is there. Look around to see how you can live your dreams without the title, praise, or compensation. Look around to see how you can *be* the blessing you desire.

You may feel weary from doing the work, going out of your way, or always showing up for others, but I promise that what you make happen for others, God will make happen for you. And not as a reward but because you are finally doing what you were always called to do. You are finally living in alignment, and from that, blessings flow. So don't grow weary of being a blessing or always being the one to make it happen. It's part of the process of receiving.

Make your dreams a reality. Find out what activities put you in alignment with your highest self, bless your community with those talents, then let God honor you. Let Him bless your commitment and obedience. Because you deserve everything you prayed for, in this life and the next.

Affirmation: What you make happen for others, God will make happen for you.

Application: Draw back to this affirmation when you think what you are doing is not going to help you get to your goals. Use it to remain rooted in the fact that no experience is worthless. Your experience is helping you build capacity for your blessing. But you have to set up the environment. You have to get in formation. You do this by identifying what fulfills you, how it can fulfill others, and how you can position yourself to live in alignment. You only see the fruits of your labor when you are already living in your purpose. When we do the work without trying to gain something, we receive all that we could have ever wanted and more. Be in alignment with your purpose so your blessings can align with you.

Exploration:
1. What are you called to do? (Ignore the title and explore the talents you are meant to share.)
2. Are you using those talents?
    a. If not, what is stopping you: time, money, fear?
    b. If not, how can you learn the skills necessary to use your talents?
3. Are you contributing your talent, skills, and gifts to others while you wait?
    a. If not, what is stopping you?
4. What would it look like to be 1 percent closer to your dreams?
5. What would it look (and feel) like to be in alignment with your gifts?

How Do I Overcome Hopelessness?

Hopelessness occurs during difficult seasons. When things don't go as planned or the way you imagined, it's natural to feel discouraged. That disappointment is your mind's way of signaling that something mattered to you. That's okay. You're not a failure. You're simply being redirected to what matters more.

It can occur during isolation. When you feel you have failed, lost, or can't go on, don't try to figure it out on your own. You don't have all the answers, Sway. You need help. You need a different perspective. A fresh perspective won't come from sitting alone with your thoughts, favorite snacks, and green tea on vacation. (This is my truth. Insert your own.)

Instead, meet hopelessness with company, compassion, and curiosity. Be honest with your community about how you feel. Let them support your mental health and give you a different point of view because your truth isn't the only truth. Once you hear another perspective, have compassion for the version of you that no longer exists and the one that is forming. Appreciate all you have learned along the way so you are no longer starting from scratch, but experience. Then, lean into what's next.

Those doors closed so you could explore new paths with courage, clarity, and strength. Because your purpose was never tied to a single outcome. And losing one path was never going to stop your shine. It was never going to erase the plans He has for you. If anything, things not working out was your blessing! So, get curious about how good life can get. Start to move as if everything is working out for you—because it is!

You balance hopelessness by remembering that everything has meaning and purpose. It loses its grip when you recognize that closed doors are not failures but divine detours. Stay open, visible, and expectant. Your story isn't over. It's being rewritten with greater depth, purpose, and promise.

(Now, hold my hand.)

You are the reason.

SUMMARY

Well, you made it through some really tough parts—for me and you. I hope you paused, laughed, cried, and saw how complex, but beautiful, life is. No matter where these pages took you, I hope you've found a mirror in them: a reflection of your strength, struggle, and spirit. This book wasn't written to tell you who to be. It was written to remind you of who you already are.

Throughout this journey, I've shared the tools and language that gave me the capacity to hold heavy emotions. These weren't lessons learned in theory. They were earned in heartbreak, therapy, prayer, community, and quiet moments when I finally told myself the truth. And now, I offer them to you, not as prescriptions but as possibilities. It's possible to have healthy, fulfilling relationships. It's possible to feel your emotions without them taking control of your life. And it's possible to go through these journeys and become more yourself.

Navigating Relationships

Navigating relationships doesn't get easier with time. There's always something you don't know about others or yourself. While books, podcasts, and therapy can introduce new ideas and frameworks, they can't do the work for you. Instead, these mediums can help you conceptualize what is going on more objectively. They are resources to help you see things in the past better, but more work is needed to get it right in the moment. Time and effort are needed for successful relationships.

Before you are able to hold emotions that come up, you have to be willing to be seen, corrected, and loved by others completely. It's not natural to know how to do these things. They have to be learned, not by reading or listening but by doing. You get relationships right when you *practice* relating to others, again and again. That looks like:

- Talking through discomfort versus creating false narratives about intentions

- Remembering no relationship is too sacred to be held accountable

- Establishing and practicing boundaries in safe spaces

- Building the capacity to communicate your emotions and needs

- Letting go of what the relationship *used* to be and embracing what it *actually* is

- Showing up when it's needed and not just convenient

- Healing your past traumas and generational curses

- Allowing others to be a mirror *to* you and *for* you

- Growing *together.*

None of these actions is easy. It takes time, patience, and a lot of energy to be in reciprocal relationships. But you get to decide who to share that energy with. You get to decide who you want to build, unlearn, redefine, and reestablish your trust, safety, and communication with. You get to decide! So, don't take those decisions lightly. Choose carefully who you want to be a mirror for you. Then let them. Let them tell you how beautiful you are. Let them remind you how talented you are. Let them show you that you are more than enough—for them and for you.

Balancing Emotions

Even when your emotions feel everywhere, you are in control. *You* have the power to notice, acknowledge, and care for them. Because that's what they need. They need your undivided attention. So, listen up. They won't wait until it's convenient for you to speak.

Instead, grief will catch you off guard. Anxiety will tighten your chest. Anger will threaten to spill over into every relationship. Control will scare you. Fear will isolate you. Self-doubt will lie about your abilities. And hopelessness will send you to dark places.

Don't let it. Emotions are journeys, not final destinations. Don't let them put a period where a comma is supposed to be. Don't let them have the final say on how things are going to end. You have a way through now.

Instead of fixing, numbing, or avoiding your feelings, acknowledge and care for them. Communicate with others that they are in the room too. Allow for others to see you wholly and not just "at your best." (You don't serve anyone by acting like parts of you don't exist.) Then, hold your emotions. Allow them to breathe in the presence of others or through journaling. Validate their presence with the affirmations you learned or a "yes, and" statement.

You heard that right. If you are mad, *be* mad *and* communicate why. You can say, "I am mad that you lied to me, *and* I would like to see a deeper commitment to your word." Feel the emotion and communicate how it makes you feel. Yes, I have this emotion, *and* this is what I would like to happen, or what I was expecting, or how it made me feel.

Communicating emotions doesn't make you weak, emotional, or sensitive. It makes you human and relatable. It makes it easier to get what you need, even if that's just to be seen or heard. Don't apologize for that. And don't run away from that, either.

Because there's someone willing to hold you *and* your emotions with care. There is someone who wants to remind you that you are not the negative things your mind tries to make you believe. There is someone deeply wanting to tell you that they feel the same way and they want to walk through the valleys alongside you. Allow them. Let them remind you of your humanity, normality, and divinity. Let them hear and hold your emotions with care. Then say what you need. After all, that is where healing lives—in the daily choice to *be* and express yourself.

Becoming Yourself

Your best self was always within reach. It didn't need to be found; it needed to be accessed. You access who you truly are by being present with your truths, not by doing more to become like every-one else. Access comes when you take an honest look at where you are in life (emotionally, financially, spiritually, or physically) and decide whether you want to stay there. It's a daily reflection and decision.

If you go beyond the labels and titles that can't express the fullness of your identity, who are you? Who do you want to be? What do you want to do? Do you show up as that? Are you okay with that?

At any point, you can decide to be something else. You can decide to be *someone* else. And you *are*! Every ah-ha moment, experience, and conversation changes your view on life. It changes your perspective on how life can go and how good it can get. That is where your ideal self is born. That is where your fire-burning desire and determination to access her is born.

And you finally have the resources to do so. Your ideal self can be accessed through tools, affirmations, and capacity. Whether you are using the Self-Care Pyramid to access what you need when life gets busy, the Work Breakdown Structure to define your work boundaries, the Community Map to define what community looks like to you, or simply establishing boundaries in your relationships, you can connect with your authentic self when it matters most. So, tap in!

There's a version of you that wants to stop shrinking to fit into rooms you have outgrown. One that wants to pour from a full cup. She is no longer trying to get by unscathed by life and others. She is committed to accessing every good thing this world has to offer. Tap into her.

You're ready.

Finally, a Piece of Peace

You found it. You found the capacity to make authentic decisions when it comes to navigating relationships, balancing emotions, and becoming yourself. It wasn't easy, but you did it. And now, you can finally rest. Prop up your feet in your favorite chair, with your favorite beverage, and take a load off.

You've found many moments that allowed you to reflect, laugh, and breathe. Moments that showed you that who you are is more than enough. Above all, you found a piece of peace.

Sit with that. You saw what you tried to hide from. And still you committed to letting go of the titles, labels, and self-soothing methods you once clung to for safety. You rejected the idea that you have to be someone else to be valued. And more importantly, you let go of the notion that you should do this journey alone.

I'm *so* proud of you. You did it. No, you did *that*!

In all of this, you found that peace comes from realizing you were never stuck; you were misaligned. You were never broken; you were becoming. And you were never lost; you were finding your way through.

(Now, hold my hand.)

Welcome home.

AFTERWORD

When I wrote this, I didn't have the answers. Actually, I wrote this at a time when I was looking for answers. I was searching for ways to overcome the emotions we explored together. Without a clear direction for the book, I poured what I've been through and what I've learned onto these pages.

In the end, I saw so many different versions of myself. They weren't all pretty, but they were honest and real. I saw everything I tried to bury, and the truth that couldn't stay away. I released who I thought I was to see who I really am more clearly. It was hard, but I was blessed enough to have a community to call me in when my doubts were greater than my victories, my fears were greater than my faith, and my trauma was greater than my hope.

This book came with immense pain. It came after I wanted to discontinue my own story. Yet, that wasn't in His divine plan. In the midst of pain, my community reminded me that I still had a story—one that was worth sharing. One that was worth *living*.

No matter how hard it feels, this is just a piece of your story, too. No matter how difficult the relationships get, they are the structures in which you will survive. Build them carefully and intentionally. Allow them to give you a piece of peace.

My hope is that you saw yourself, you saw a way through, and you found something to hold on to. I pray that these words inspire you to live the life of your dreams. More importantly, I pray you continue to exist, and ultimately thrive, by your own standards, no one else's.

With each page, let this book be a reminder that you are strong, powerful, intelligent, beautiful, healing, and the source of all good things. Let it remind you that it ain't on you, it's in you. Whatever you are seeking will find you, too.

I invite you to explore your truth even more deeply with *Finally, A Piece of Peace Guidebook*. I created it for those moments when life feels heavy and you need some space to breathe. Use it to tell your story. Use it to define your standards. Use it to affirm what I already know is true: You're iconic, a legend, and the world would be nothing without you!

Now, drop your shoulders, unclench your jaw, and take a *deep* breath.

(Holding your own hand.)

You are your piece of peace.

ACKNOWLEDGEMENTS

This book would not be what it is without my community. These moments of radical honesty would not be as relatable if I didn't have feedback from people I knew and people I didn't. Their reminders to remain vulnerable about how I navigated sitting with myself, and others made this my favorite work of art. I'm so grateful for:

Courtney: I don't think you realize how much of a blessing you are. I almost paused my author journey because editing felt too long and arduous. But you showed me how to fall in love with the process. You reminded me that I wasn't doing this alone. Now, I am a better writer, reader, and learner. Thank you for sharing your gifts with me. This book would not be as transformative without you.

Aemilia: Thank you for reminding me that my story needs to breathe, just like I do. In the moments where I intellectualized my emotions, you reminded me to slow down and give weight to my story.

Tess: Thank you for translating the emotions of the book to the cover design. This is the first impression for the readers, and you made us all feel something. I'm grateful for your patience, creativity, and craft. It's unreal!

Fata: Thank you for always creating space for authors to tell their truths. It inspired me and helped me not feel alone during this journey. Now, author to author, you gave me feedback that no one else did. You approached the book with the target audience in mind. I'm so grateful for you seeing, teaching, and supporting me. It's made all the difference in my writing journey.

Jasmine: Thank you for giving me a fresh, and honest perspective about my work. Your reminder that I, "wrote from the heart, and not the mind," was all the reassurance I needed to feel comfortable being vulnerable throughout these pages. I'm grateful for your opinion and willingness to share this project as if it were your own. Your constant support means more than you know.

Jazzmine: Thank you for being the first person to see me fully. For a long time, you have reminded me who I am in this world, who I am to others and who I am to God. This was another example of how you show up for me in every season and for any reason. I'm so grateful for your honesty, guidance, and love.

Addie: Thank you for sitting in these pages with me and reminding me that life happens to all of us, but how we show up for others and ourselves will make all the difference. Thank you for reminding me that even the heaviest stories will resonate and help someone through. I'm so grateful for you.

Tiffany: Thank you for sharing your time and heart with me. You validated that my words weren't too emotional; they were honest.

You validated that this was important work that needed to be shared. But most importantly you validated that I was seen and heard in these pages. I'm grateful for your input that made this book what it is today.

Haile: Thank you for your standing in my truths with me. Hearing your feedback reminded me that my voice can be heard, and the words can connect with the audience regardless if they know me deeply or not. It was all the validation I needed that being vulnerable with a wider audience was not only okay but celebrated. Thank you for seeing me.

Brittany: Thank you for always supporting me in this journey and life. It was never "why" do you want to live your dreams, and always "when" are you going to live your dreams. Thank you for listening to hours of voice notes as I read to you early versions of these pages and for encouraging me to keep going as I navigated healing and storytelling. I'm grateful for you.

Nathalie: Thank you for making these affirmations your own. Over time, hearing you reference my words back to me reminded me just how powerful these words are. I love seeing my life reflected through your eyes. Thank you for answering late night texts and voice messages on how these stories sound, impact the reader, and what was still missing. Your opinion will always mean the most to me.

Cortney: From the beginning, you told me this was something special. When I read my first chapters to you, I saw you laugh when I laughed. I watched you cry when I cried. That was the moment I knew this book would be more than a healing exercise for me, but my evidence for, "how good it can get." Thank you for reminding me to see this through. Thank you for treating this book as your own. It would not be here without your feedback, friendship, and support. You're one of one.

AFFIRMATIONS

SOURCES

Chandler, Zai. "Someone's Talking About You." You-Tube, uploaded by Zai Chandler, 2024, www.youtube.com/watch?v=rUE5kKS8-BQ.

Merriam-Webster.com Dictionary, Merriam-Webster, https://www.merriam-webster.com/dictionary/peace. Accessed 1 Dec. 2025.

Roberts, Sarah Jakes. "The Undoing." YouTube, uploaded by The Potter's House of Dallas, 11 July 2021, www.youtube.com/watch?v=K7r09B95zC0.

Wiest, Brianna. *The Mountain Is You: Transforming Self-Sabotage into Self-Mastery.* Thought Catalog Books, 2020. pp. 98–100.

Williamson, Marianne. *The Law of Divine Compensation: On Work, Money, and Miracles.* Narrated by Marianne Williamson, Harper-Audio, 2012. Audible, www.audible.com.

RESOURCES

This book was inspired by many questions or thoughts that were explored in other resources. I hope you read, listen, and view them for yourself. May they inspire the author in you too.

Books:

Law of Divine Compensation by Marianne Williamson

Boundaries by Dr Henry Cloud, Chris Tompson, and John Townsend

Set Boundaries, Find Peace by Nedra Glover Tawwab

The Mountain Is You by Brianna Wiest

Wherever You Go, There You Are by Jon Kabat-Zinn

Finally, a Piece of Peace Guidebook by Ja'Mara Washington (Coming June 2026)

Sermons:

The Undoing by Sarah Jakes Roberts

Someone's Talking About You by Zai Chandler

Music:

I carefully curated a Spotify playlist for you to listen to as you enjoy this book. It is equipped with songs referenced in the book as well as songs that were relatable to the experiences within the affirmations. The playlist includes alternative, alternative R&B, neo-soul, afro-house, hip-hop, gospel, and gospel rap. You can listen while you read, in-between readings or after you have found your piece of peace. Either way, they will help you feel more connected to the stories and your truths.

Community:
Instagram: @finallyapieceofpeace
Substack: Heard and Held
Virtual Book Club: Finally, a Piece of Peace

ABOUT THE AUTHOR

Photograph By: Alexis Akarolo

Ja'Mara Washington is an author and wellness advocate whose work blends raw storytelling, humor, and practical tools for healing. In her debut book, *Finally, a Piece of Peace,* she draws on her Southern roots, faith, and personal journey through grief, self-doubt, and reinvention to guide readers toward balance and self-discovery. Her work has helped women across the country feel safe, seen and loved again.

When she is not writing, Ja'Mara enjoys deep conversations, specialty coffee shops, biking, traveling and annoying her four-year-old cat. She is a Florida native based in Washington, DC.

Connect and discover more of her work at:
www.jamarawashington.com

www.ingramcontent.com/pod-product-compliance
Lightning Source LLC
Chambersburg PA
CBHW020306150626
46552CB00022B/1766